London's City Churches

by Stephen Millar

London's City Churches

Written by Stephen Millar
Photography by Stephen Millar
Edited by Abigail Willis
Design by Susi Koch & Lesley Gilmour
Maps by Lesley Gilmour
Cover Design by The Partners

Published 2006 by

Metro Publications
PO Box 6336
London
N1 6PY

Printed and bound in India
© Metro Publication 2006

British Library Cataloguing in Publication Data.
A catalogue record for this book is available from the British Library.

ISBN 1 902910 24 9

for Bill Millar, Helen,
Patrick, Annapurna
and Blythe

Acknowledgements

My thanks to Dr Diane Atkinson, Gillian Blachford and Michael Coles for their help in reviewing parts of the text.

Metro Publications would like to thank Trish, Jack, Bob and all those at The Partners that have contributed to the design of our new covers and logo.

Contents

Introduction 1

Area Map 12

City Churches 14

Towers 168

City Churches Walks...172

Appendix 192

   Wren Churches 192

   Useful Addresses 193

   Glossary of Church Architecture 194

   Bibliography 195

Index..196

EIKON
BASI-
LIKE

St Katherine Cree

Introduction

The City churches within London's 'Square Mile' represent one of the most concentrated and impressive set of ecclesiastical buildings in existence. Famously, many are creations by Sir Christopher Wren following the destruction caused by the Great Fire of London in 1666, although there are several survivors from other eras that are often overlooked. The evolution of the City churches is synonymous with the history of London itself – long lost origins during the Roman period, sparks of life in the Dark Ages, then a gradual transformation from wood to ragstone and then marble as London came first to European then global prominence.

Before London spread west or out to the suburbs, the City was London. Contained within old Roman walls that could be circumnavigated in the space of an hour, its monasteries, churches and prisons, mayors, writers and businessmen had a huge influence over the cultural and political life of the country. Even the monarch could not enter the City without permission.

This influence peaked in the 17th century when the list of notable people associated with the City churches reads like a 'who's who' of English social, artistic and political history, including Shakespeare, Charles I, Pepys, Defoe, Evelyn, Hooke, Wren, Judge Jeffreys, Inigo Jones, and Archbishop Laud. In the following centuries the rich and famous increasingly chose to live outside the crowded City walls. The advent of industrialisation and the railways encouraged many ordinary people to live outside the City and commute back to their jobs for the first time. As a result, whilst the City prospered economically, something significant had been lost in terms of the vibrancy of its religious communities. The churches were reduced in stature, gradually being abandoned by their old congregations who now lived in Norwood or Kensington rather than on Fleet Street or Bishopsgate. By the 20th century the remaining churches served a dwindling City population of a few thousand instead of a few hundred thousand and those churches lucky enough to survive the savage destruction of the Blitz have subsequently taken different paths. Inevitably some have become little more than museums, largely empty except for Christmas carol concerts, although still serving as a testament to what the City used to be and shall never be again. Others have taken up the challenge more aggressively and are active places, doing their utmost to get people through the door. A church is after all just a building and it is the people who congregate within it who decide what purpose it should serve.

There remain many people dedicated to increasing public awareness of the City churches and preserving their history, most notably the 'Friends of the City Churches' – without whom many of the churches would hardly be accessible to the public at all. The Friends provide helpers for an increasing number of churches during the week when the church would otherwise be unstaffed and closed to the public. The Friends also host an annual walk around the City churches when some buildings normally closed are opened for the day (see page 193).

Roman and Saxon Origins

The story of the City churches really begins with the Roman Empire. The Romans initially settled the area that we now know as the City as a military camp. However by the end of the 1st century AD 'Londinium' was the political and economic capital of the country, with perhaps 30,000 inhabitants. The later Roman Empire converted to Christianity, however there is little evidence in the City of any churches from that period, despite the claims of St Peter Cornhill. In fact the only material discovery of a Roman place of worship has been of a 3rd-century temple to Mithras by the Walbrook stream. Christianity, whilst perhaps not universally popular or practised, was established and in the 4th century Restitutus was recorded as the Bishop of London when attending the Council of Arles at the command of Emperor Constantine.

The Romans built a great fortified wall around their settlement, marking the boundaries of what would become known as the 'City'. The reinforcement of these fortifications reflected the growing instability of an Empire that was on the wane – the Romans effectively left London to fend for itself c.410 AD. The City fell prey to raids by both Angles and Saxons, however it is not clear whether the area within the Roman walls was largely abandoned because of these threats or, more likely, the remaining inhabitants did not have the expertise to prevent a sophisticated Roman city of temples, forums, bathhouses and complex plumbing from rotting away. This must have been a strange time as those who remembered the Roman Empire had to resort to clambering over its structures in order to salvage materials to build much more modest dwellings. By the mid 4th century AD most of Britain had probably accepted Saxon rule, with London under Saxon control no later than the mid 6th century AD. The Saxons settled largely in an area outside the old City walls between Covent Garden and the Thames, and the population of the old Roman city was probably tiny compared to the days of Empire.

In the late 6th century AD the resurgence of the Christian faith in Rome and Ireland led to missions to pagan Britain. Christianity slowly began to reassert itself, particularly after St Augustine's visit in 596 AD. In 601 AD Pope Gregory proclaimed London the main bishopric in Britain and in 604 AD Ethelbert, King of Kent, began construction of the first St Paul's Cathedral. Around this time Mellitus was declared Bishop of London by Augustine, now Archbishop of Britain, and Christianity became once more the official religion for Londoners. Whilst records of this period of the 'Dark Ages' are scant, it appears the population was still not fully converted – a process that was to take some considerable time. London later came under attack from the Danes in the 9th century, with Alfred the Great leading the Anglo-Saxon resistance. He eventually recaptured London from the Danes in c.886 AD and set about renovating the largely empty City and rebuilding its fortifications.

Many residents of Saxon Lundenwic withdrew for safety within the repaired City walls marking the first mass inhabitation since Roman times. Whilst the Danes threatened the City for some time, and even occupied it once more in the early 11th century, stability of a kind began to return. It is from this period that evidence of the first City churches begins to emerge, for example the Saxon remains discovered at All Hallows by the Tower, St Bride's and St Alban Wood Street.

Medieval Period

Slowly wooden chapels were upgraded to stone. After the Norman Conquest of 1066, the new rulers introduced a more sophisticated culture of keeping documentary records and it is from the 11th and 12th centuries that many City churches are first recorded, even though their dedications to popular Saxon saints (such as St Olave, St Edmund, St Dunstan or St Botolph) suggest they were founded much earlier. The Normans built the crypt of St-Mary-le-Bow in the late 11th century, and their Gothic influence can also be seen in the remains of the Norman choir in St Bartholomew the Great (c.1123), and the Temple Church (consecrated 1185). The great religious orders also began to lay down their foundations within the City, the principal houses being the Crutched Friars, the Greyfriars, the Blackfriars, St Mary le Grand, the Priory of the Holy Trinity, the Priory of St Bartholomew, the Priory of St Helen and the Abbey of St Clare. These orders (including the Knights Templar at Temple Church) dominated religious life within the City and many of today's churches such as St Bartholomew the Great, the Dutch Church and St Helen's owe their existence to these long-lost priories.

By the late Middle Ages there were around 110 parish churches within the City. The parallel development of the great religious houses and the parishes is well illustrated in the history of St Helen's. The original building just consisted of a parish church until a nunnery was set up alongside. Two separate churches continued side by side until combined as a single parish church after the Reformation in the 16th century. An example of the differences between these two developments can be seen today by comparing the grandeur of St Bartholomew the Great, part of the great Priory, with the tiny parish church of St Ethelburga, clearly built from much more modest funds.

Many of the old churches were rebuilt right up until the late medieval period, and examples of this can be seen in the tower of St Katherine Cree (c.1504), St Andrew Undershaft (c.1530) and St Giles (c.1545). New ragstone was used, rather than the remnants of Roman buildings as had been the practice in the construction of earlier Saxon churches. From the 14th century, towers were increasingly built on the west end to house belfries. Interiors became more ornate, and from this period we see an increasing number of fine monuments such as the tomb of Rahere in St Bartholomew the Great, the many tombs inside St Helen's, or the brasses in All Hallows by the Tower.

The Reformation

When Henry VIII decided to break with Rome, one major conse-quence was the Dissolution of the Monasteries in the 1530s. This was, aside from the Great Fire, the Blitz, and Victorian demolitions, the single biggest event to impact the City churches. The King's onslaught on the monastic orders resulted in most of the great abbeys within the City walls being turned over to secular use. In some cases such as St Bartholomew the Great, St Bartholomew the Less, Christ Church Newgate, and St Helen's, a truncated survival of some kind took place as the local congregation absorbed part of the abandoned buildings to form a new parish church. The parish churches were also fundamentally altered as the bright colours and symbolic objects so beloved of the Roman Catholic church were covered in lime-wash or stripped away. These included the vividly painted rood screens and walls, the statues and, in the case of St Andrew Undershaft, the maypole that had stood outside the church for centuries but which was chopped up and burnt after being denounced as a 'heathen idol'. But perhaps the biggest change for the parishioners was the banishment of the old ceremonies with their colour and drama that had dictated religious life for centuries.

The impact of the Reformation meant that by the early 17th century many churches were in a state of neglect. There was a revival in church building in the 1620-30s under the sponsorship of William Laud, Bishop of London and later Archbishop of Canterbury. More than half the City churches underwent some kind of repair, and Laud himself consecrated the reconstructed St Katherine Cree. St Katherine's, with its unique mix of classical and Gothic architecture, is the single most important example of church building from this era. This was also the time of the first 'celebrity' architects, such as Inigo Jones who worked on the restoration of old St Paul's, and who possibly acted as consultant on many church renovations of the time. The furnishings inside the churches also benefited from this revival, one good example being the fine font dating from 1634 by master mason Nicholas Stone in St Andrew Undershaft. The City churchyards were also improved with elaborate 'memento mori', such as the skulls dramatically depicted above the entrance of the churchyard of St Olave Hart Street that later made such an impression on Charles Dickens.

The Great Fire of 1666

The famous fire that started in a baker's shop in Pudding Lane lasted for five days, gutting the medieval City. The statistics are staggering – 13,000 houses were destroyed, as were four-fifths of all buildings. Out of 107 parish churches 85 were burnt, and nearly 450 acres of ground laid waste. Perhaps more incredible was the fact that out of a population of more than 150,000 made homeless only six deaths were recorded. Various plans were put forward for the reconstruction of the City, including radical ones drawn up by Wren and Pepys' fellow diarist John Evelyn. Given the politics involved, with everyone from the King to the officers of the decimated parishes wanting their own say, the result was unsurprisingly a compromise. The old City could never be reconstructed as it was, however the opportunity to produce a modern layout was not taken either. One third of a new coal tax was put aside for the reconstruction of the parish churches, with another third earmarked for St Paul's Cathedral. The task for this work was entrusted to Sir Christopher Wren (1632-1723) and under his supervision 51 new churches were eventually built, all on the same site as their predecessors. Today, 24 Wren parish churches remain, together with six towers.

Wren was talented in many ways other than architecture, both co-founding The Royal Society and serving as a professor of astronomy at Oxford. Architecture was initially only a side-line for him, and he owed his early success as much to patronage as to talent. He had already been involved in considering the renovation of old St Paul's when the Great Fire broke out, and though his intelligent plans for the new City were not adopted he nevertheless impressed the authorities so much that he was chosen to lead the six man commission that would supervise the reconstruction of the parish churches and St Paul's Cathedral. Whilst Wren was personally involved in all 51 designs, he was ably helped by some of the most gifted men of his generation. These included Robert Hooke (1635-1703), scientist and professor of geometry at Gresham College, whose *Micrographia* (1665) was the first extensive account of the microscopic world. Another was Nicholas Hawksmoor (1661-1736), who worked for Wren until the great architect retired, and then himself built several churches in London. Hawksmoor also worked with Sir John Vanbrugh on Blenheim Palace and Castle Howard. Wren assembled a team of fine master craftsmen including the eminent Grinling Gibbons (1648-1721). Gibbons was born in Rotterdam and became Master Carver to the Crown. Such is Gibbons' reputation that many church's claim their font cover or reredos is his work, although few are able to prove it (see St Mary Abchurch, page 111).

Wren was paid for working on St Paul's Cathedral, but not for the parish churches. In the latter case the construction and financing was a matter of discussion and negotiation between Wren and the individual parishes. Some, such as the parishioners of St Sepulchre's, grew frustrated with Wren's delay in starting work and instead organised the rebuilding themselves. Other parishes, such as the Gothic St Mary Aldermary, may have imposed conditions that resulted in Wren rebuilding a church on its existing lines that was not perhaps to his classical taste. In many cases Wren was restricted to the confines of the former church site, either because of surrounding buildings that had to be respected or the need to incorporate substantial ruins of the old church. This may explain why some of his churches look quite plain from the outside, but contain such treasures inside, the contrast being most marked at St Stephen Walbrook. Much of the day-to-day work was carried out by Wren's assistants, leaving Wren free to concentrate on St Paul's. By the end of the 1680s most of the main rebuilding had been completed although many towers and steeples were added slightly later.

Wren aimed to build proper Protestant churches, however since the Reformation very few had been built in the City. He looked for inspiration to Europe, particularly Calvinist Holland. This explains why some Wren churches such as St Benet's, St Martin Ludgate, and St Mary Abchurch are described as having a 'Dutch' feel. Wren wanted his churches to avoid the ornate clutter of a Roman Catholic building and resulting in his extensive use of galleries so the congregation could see and hear everything that was going on. Wren also spent a great deal of time planning the furnishings inside the churches – the reredoses, fonts, pulpits, screens, and organs that survive from this era are of a quality that has never been surpassed.

After Wren

Wren's assistant Hawksmoor continued his master's legacy with St Mary Woolnoth (completed 1727), and later 18th-century rebuilding took place under eminent architects such as George Dance the Elder (St Botolph Aldgate), George Dance the Younger (All Hallows London Wall, St Bartholomew the Less), and James Gould (St Botolph Bishopsgate). St Dunstan in the West is a fine example of an early 19th-century Gothic styled building, but standards were not maintained during the Victorian age. This is unsurprising given that from the mid 19th century the City population began to decline as the new railways lured people out to the suburbs. Parishes that once had thousands of inhabitants became largely abandoned and so the churches began to lose their relevance. In 1841 the population of the City stood at approximately 125,000 however by 1901 it was just over 25,000.

The tide had truly turned for the City churches and now demolitions began to take place. This was formalised by the Union of Benefices Act of 1860 that allowed the Church authorities for the first time to sell redundant churches, with the proceeds often being used to finance the building of churches in the new suburbs. At the same time thriving City institutions needed more space on which to build new office blocks so the Church found no shortage of buyers for their land. The demolitions continued at speed until the early 20th century at which point around 20 churches had been lost. Whilst less well known and less dramatic than the destruction caused by the Blitz, in some ways these demolitions were just as tragic for the City churches. The Victorians did not stop at demolishing churches – they also took to extensively renovating them and have often been criticised for their heavy-handed changes. One major transformation was of St Michael Cornhill by Sir George Gilbert Scott c.1860 into essentially a Victorian church. All this while there was little new building, one exception being St Mary Moorfields (RC) by George Sherrin, completed in 1903.

The Blitz of 1940-41 resulted in 23 of the 49 remaining Anglican City churches being badly damaged or destroyed. Five were never rebuilt (St Stephen Coleman, St Mildred Bread Street, St Swithin Cannon Street, St Mary Aldermanbury, and Holy Trinity Minories). St Alban's and St Augustine's survive with their towers only remaining, whilst the substantial remains of St Dunstan in the East and Christchurch Newgate can still be visited. St Mary Aldermanbury was demolished but later reconstructed in Fulton, Missouri USA in the 1960s. Two modern non-Anglican churches were built to replace the destroyed Dutch Church, Austin Friars and the Jewin Welsh Church. The remaining Anglican churches were restored, and reopened over a number of years following Second World War, the degree of reconstruction depending both on the extent of the damage and the personal style of architect employed. The restored St Anne and St Agnes now appears similar to how it would have done to Wren, his typically large clear-glass windows illuminating fine woodwork that in fact comes from other destroyed Wren churches. Others, such as St Mary le Bow, St Bride's and St Andrew by the Wardrobe, have a much more modern feel about them. Very few churches or places of worship can honestly say they remain largely unaltered since Wren's era, although St Benet's is the chief claimant and, oddly enough, another is The Spanish and Portuguese Synagogue (not built by Wren but employing many of his craftsmen). St Mary at Hill was largely unchanged before a terrible fire in 1988 gutted the building, and St Ethelburga's was a prime example of a surviving medieval church until an IRA bomb in 1993 caused enormous damage.

Since the post-Second World War restorations there has been little new church building of note in the City in respect of the 39 surviving Anglican churches, although the rebuilding of St Ethelburga's in the 1990s was a commendable success. Perhaps the most striking addition has been the massive Travertine altar carved by Henry Moore that was controversially introduced to one of Wren's masterpieces, St Stephen Walbrook.

St Andrew by the Wardrobe

Note

Throughout the Guide I use the convention of giving directions based upon the altar being on the east end of the church. The visiting times are correct at the time of publication however they frequently change and it is always sensible to call the church to get the latest information. Church contact details can be accessed through City Events and The Friends of the City Churches (see page 193 for details).

London's City Churches Map

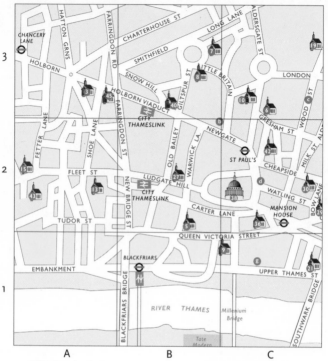

1. All Hallows by the Tower F:1
2. All Hallows on the Wall E:3
3. St Andrew Holborn A:3
4. St Andrew Undershaft F:2
5. St Andrew by the Wardrobe B:2
6. St Anne and St Agnes C:3
7. St Bartholomew the Great B:3
8. St Bartholomew the Less B:3
9. St Benet Paul's Wharf C:1
10. St Botolph without Aldersgate C:3
11. St Botolph without Aldgate F:2
12. St Botolph without Bishopsgate E:3
13. St Bride's Fleet Street A:2
14. St Clement Eastcheap E:1

15. St Dunstan in the West A:2
16. The Dutch Church, Austin Friars E:2
17. St Edmund the King and Martyr E:2
18. St Ethelburga the Virgin E:2
19. St Giles Cripplegate C:3
20. St Helen Bishopsgate E:2
21. St James Garlickhythe C:1
22. St Katherine Cree F:2
23. St Lawrence Jewry D:2
24. St Magnus the Martyr E:1
25. St Margaret Lothbury D:2
26. St Margaret Pattens E:1
27. St Martin within Ludgate B:2
28. St Mary Abchurch D:1

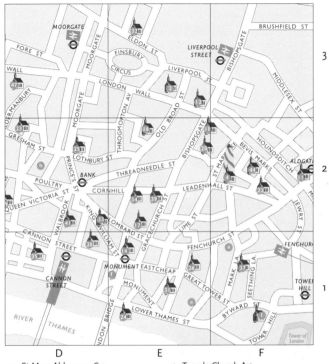

29. St Mary Aldermary C:2
30. St Mary le Bow C:2
31. St Mary at Hill E:1
32. St Mary Moorfields E:3
33. St Mary Woolnoth D:2
34. St Michael Cornhill E:2
35. St Michael Paternoster Royal D:1
36. St Nicholas Cole Abbey C:2
37. St Olave Hart Street F:1
38. St Paul's Cathedral C:2
39. St Peter upon Cornhill E:2
40. St Sepulchre without Newgate B:3
41. St Stephen Walbrook D:2
42. St Vedast alias Foster C:2

43. Temple Church A:2
44. Spanish & Portuguese Synagogue F:2
45. The City Temple A:3
46. Jewin Welsh Church (off map)
47. St Mary Aldermanbury D:3

a. All Hallows Staining F:1
b. Christ Church Newgate B:2
c. St Alban Wood St C:3
d. St Augustine with St Faith C:2
e. St Dunstan in the East E:1
f. St Martin Orgar E:1
g. St Mary Somerset C:1
h. St Olave Jewry D:2

City Churches

All Hallows by the Tower

1. All Hallows by the Tower

Saxon church; rebuilt in medieval period; rebuilt 17th century
and escaped Great Fire but gutted in Blitz; reopened 1957

Situated beside the Tower of London, All Hallows (or 'All Saints')
stands somewhat stranded between a busy ring road and a new glass
and steel office block. Much of the original church was destroyed
during the Blitz, however its history and remaining treasures are
exceptional. Until recently it was known as 'All Hallows Barking',
a reference to Barking Abbey in Essex founded in the 7th century
AD by St Erkenweld, 4th Bishop of London, for his sister St
Ethelburga. The Abbey owned the land upon which All Hallows
was built in around 675 AD, and continued to supply the vicars to
the church until the Dissolution of the Monasteries. The Blitz gutted the church, but also revealed All Hallows' Roman and Anglo-
Saxon foundations that pre-date the Tower by 400 years – making
this one of the earliest Christian sites in London. Part of the 15th-
century structure survives despite damage done by a huge gunpow-
der explosion nearby in 1650. Oliver Cromwell sponsored the subsequent reconstruction and Pepys climbed the new tower to
observe the Great Fire of 1666, recording that he went 'up to the
top of Barkeing steeple, and there was the saddest sight of desola-
tion that I ever saw. Everywhere great fires, the fire being spread as
far as I could see it.' Scorch marks from the fire could still be seen
on the stone around the church entrance up until the Blitz.

The interior is largely a post-Second World War reconstruction.
As you enter, look out for the vestry on the right which contains
an original Saxon arch full of Roman tiles salvaged from the ruins
of the Imperial city and hidden under plaster until the Blitz. Walk
past this to reach steps leading down to the fascinating 14th-centu-
ry basement undercroft which contains a small museum. Just as you
descend a Roman tessellated pavement (c.1st century AD) can be
seen to the left, and further along are remains of three Saxon cross-
es. Straight ahead is a stone altar taken from the Templars' castle of
Atlit that was situated on Mount Carmel in Israel, and one of the

last Crusader strongholds to fall in the 13th century. The Knights Templar were connected to the Chapel of St Mary which once stood beside the church, and it is rumoured some Templar knights are buried in the undercroft itself. There are now three chapels in the undercroft and the location of the chapel of St Francis was only rediscovered in 1925 after lying hidden for several centuries. There is also a memorial to William Penn, English Quaker and founder of the American State of Pennsylvania. Penn was baptized here in 1644, the font later given to Christ Church in Philadelphia in 1697 where it can still be found today. Penn was imprisoned in the Tower nearby for publishing controversial religious pamphlets, and his father, Admiral Penn, helped save All Hallows from the Great Fire when he organised a crucial firebreak. John Quincy Adams, sixth president of the United States (and son of the fourth president, John Adams), was married here in 1797, whilst the infamous 'Hanging' Judge Jeffreys was married here in 1667. The fascinating parish record from this era is kept on display, many of the church's records only surviving the Reformation after being hidden in a lead cistern within the tower and rediscovered in 1923.

Back up in the main building the Mariners' Chapel in the south aisle symbolizes the church's connections with the City's sea-faring past. The fascinating model ships hanging down from the ceiling were given over time in thanksgiving for safe passage, and the ledger book records the names of those lost at sea. The wood of the chapel crucifix comes from the Cutty Sark, whilst the ivory figure of Christ is said to come from the flagship of the Spanish Armada. Some furnishings survived the Blitz, including 17 brasses dating from 1389-1651 (the church has a brass rubbing centre). The beautiful lime wood font cover in the bapistry on the south-west side is attributed to Grinling Gibbons, and is one of the City's finest. Sadly, the Renatus Harris organ on which Dr Albert Schweitzer played Bach, the recording of which helped fund the Lamberene Leper colony, did not survive. The pulpit is from the 'lost' church of St Swithin's London Stone, destroyed in the Blitz.

All Hallows by the Tower

The bodies of executed prisoners were often brought here from the Tower for temporary burial, including John Fisher, Bishop of Rochester and confident of Sir Thomas More, who died in 1535 after opposing Henry VIII's Act of Succession, and Archbishop William Laud who was beheaded after being convicted of high treason in 1645. Just inside the church entrance is a modern triptych depicting Fisher and his struggles painted by Michael Coles. Post-war restoration was sympathetically carried out in a Perpendicular Gothic style by the architects Seely and Paget, the foundation stone being laid by the Queen Mother in 1948. The Wren-style spire is actually modern, although it is still an imposing sight when approached from the west along Eastcheap.

Today the church is a busy place, attracting a steady stream of tourists visiting the Tower and City workers attending the regular services.

Byward Street, EC3; Nearest transport Tower Hill LU; Open Mon-Fri 9am-6pm, Sat-Sun 10am-5pm

2. All Hallows on the Wall

First mentioned c.1130; 14th century medieval church rebuilt by George Dance the Younger in 18th century; badly damaged in Blitz and reopened 1962

All Hallows faces onto the busy traffic of London Wall, its drab, brown brick exterior suggesting an old workhouse rather than a church. In fact All Hallows was once hemmed in by the City wall to the north and other buildings to the south, with only the stuccoed western entrance designed to be appreciated by the passer-by. Today the north side of the church still stands on the foundations of the old Roman and medieval City wall. In medieval times the church was linked to the Holy Trinity Priory at Aldgate, and hermits (or 'anchorites') lived in cells built into the old City wall overlooking All Hallows. These hermits largely lived off charity, the most famous being 'Simon the Anker' who lived in a cell here for 20 years. During this time he wrote 'The Fruyt of Redempcyon', published on one of the earliest English printing presses by Wynkn de Worde near St Bride's in 1514. In the early 20th century the church provided accommodation of another kind, opening early so hundreds of office workers arriving on the cheap, early trains, had somewhere warm and dry to shelter whilst waiting for their offices to open.

Although the medieval church survived the Great Fire, it fell into disrepair and in 1765-67 was rebuilt in a Neoclassical style by George Dance the Younger, son of George Dance the Elder who designed Mansion House and St Botolph, Aldgate. George the Younger won the commission for All Hallows aged only 24 and after having recently returned from his architectural studies in Rome. His design is thought to have been influenced by the Temple of Venus in Rome and he referred to All Hallows as 'my first child'. The architect later designed Newgate Prison and Finsbury Square and was one of the four original members of the Royal Academy. In contrast to the exterior, the small interior is elegant, the lack of aisles adding to a sense of narrowness underneath a magnificent white barrel-vaulted plaster ceiling (restored by David Nye 1960-2). The striking painting behind the altar is entitled 'Ananias restoring sight to Saint Paul', and is a copy by the architect's brother of an original by Piertro da Cortona in the Church of the Conception in Rome. The black and white Portland stone and marble floor of the nave is Dance's original, whilst the 17th-century font bowl originally came from the 'lost' church of St Mary Magdalene, Old Fish Street and was later found in the crypt of St Paul's. The sword rest came from All Hallows Staining, and was used there by Sir John Rawlinson, Lord Mayor in 1753. Appropriately, Rawlinson laid the foundation stone of this church in 1765. The pair of paintings of Moses and Aaron is possibly from the pre-Dance church. The simple pulpit against the north wall was once a three-decker pulpit but has lost its lowest deck. It is unusual in that it can only be entered from the vestry that lies on the northern foundations of the old City wall rather than from the body of the church itself. Former rector S J Stone wrote the well-known church hymn *The Church's One Foundation* at the turn of the last century. Today, the church is a Guild Church meaning it no longer has parish responsibilities although it holds a regular service on the last Friday of each month. All Hallows also serves as a centre for various charitable foundations and acts as the London and South-East headquarters for Christian Aid. The Worshipful Company of Carpenters, a City Livery Company, has a historic connection to the church and for several centuries has held a service here each July.

London Wall, EC2; Nearest transport Liverpool Street LU/Rail; Open Fri 11am-3pm

All Hallows on the Wall

St Andrew Holborn

3. St Andrew Holborn

Saxon church first recorded c.959AD; rebuilt 15th century; escaped Great Fire but still rebuilt by Wren; badly damaged in Blitz and reopened 1961

Named for the Apostle, St Andrew's once stood high on Holborn Hill overlooking the Fleet River. Today the Fleet is covered over, and St Andrew's no longer appears so prominent after the ground around it was raised in 1866 to create Holborn Viaduct. The original wooden Saxon church was reworked in stone over subsequent centuries before being completely rebuilt in the mid 15th century. Rebuilding was helped by parishioner and armourer John Thavie's bequest of property to the church in 1348 and this endowment continues to play a part in the church's finances to this day.

In the 17th century St Andrew's was involved in some tumultuous events. Rector John Hackett was attacked by Puritan soldiers in 1642 whilst carrying out a baptism, surviving only through the intervention of parishioners. In 1665 the Great Plague resulted in 3,000 parishioners dying between May and October alone, although in the following year the church escaped the Great Fire because (it is said) the wind changed direction at the last minute. However the building was already dilapidated and was rebuilt by Wren in 1684-86, becoming the largest of his City parish churches. Wren preserved the 15th-century tower although it was refaced with Portland Stone c.1704. Later, the Blitz badly gutted the interior and the church only reopened in 1961 after restoration by Seely & Paget. The historical appeal of the colourful, well-lit interior is therefore somewhat limited. Just before you enter the church, look left to the north wall to see the 17th-century stone bas-relief sculpture of the Resurrection which came originally from the entrance of the Shoe Lane burial ground nearby. Around the corner on the western exterior you can also find two pretty statues of children (c.1696) that were carved by Wren's stonemason and originally came from a charity school connected to the church in Hatton Garden.

The elegant tomb of Captain Thomas Coram, founder in 1742 of the famous Foundling Hospital for abandoned children, is in the west end. It was brought here in 1961 along with the pulpit, font, and organ case after the Hospital was demolished in the 1930s. The organ was originally donated to the Hospital c.1750 by the composer George Frederick Handel, who probably played upon it during the many fund raising concerts he gave on behalf of the Hospital to fashionable London society. Prime Minister Henry Addington, Home Secretary during the infamous 'Peterloo Massacre', was christened here in 1757. Benjamin Disraeli, author and Prime Minister, was also christened here in 1817, his parents having fallen out with their local Synagogue (see Spanish and Portuguese Synagogue page 165). Marc Brunel, engineer of the first tunnel under the Thames, and father of the more famous Isambard Kingdom Brunel, was married here in 1799. William Hazlitt was married here in 1808 with Charles Lamb, another prominent essayist, as his best man. After finding a dying girl on the steps of St Andrew's one cold night in 1827, Dr William Marsden was inspired by her plight to found The Royal Free Hospital (now in Hampstead). A monument to the doctor is on the wall opposite Coram's tomb. Tragic 'boy poet' Thomas Chatterton (d.1770) was buried here after having allegedly poisoned himself aged only 17. The controversial political clergyman Dr Henry Sacheverell (d.1724) was rector here. He was buried under the high altar until his lead coffin was one of 150 stolen by the grave-digger John Lamb.

The church was no stranger to controversy – in the 18th century the church clerk was publicly pilloried after ripping out a page from the parish register of marriages in order to help another parishioner commit bigamy. Later, Charles Dickens lived nearby in Furnival's Inn whilst writing Pickwick Papers. His character Bill Sykes in *Oliver Twist* refers to St Andrew's tower clock whilst nearby Saffron Hill is said to be the setting for Fagin's Den. In summer the church's grounds are crowded with City workers, few realising that nearly 13,000 bodies once lay beneath them in the old grave-yard and crypt. Most were carried away to allow for the creation of Holborn Viaduct, however 3,000 remained until being moved as late as 2002 due to serious damp problems caused by Wren's drains becoming badly blocked. A memorial at Manor Park cemetery remembers the dead who have been reburied there. Today, St Andrew's is a Guild Church and until recently housed the Royal College of Organists.

Holborn Circus, EC4; Nearest transport Chancery Lane LU (closed Sunday); Open Mon-Fri 9am-5pm

St Andrew Holborn

St Andrew Undershaft

4. St Andrew Undershaft

First recorded early 12th century; rebuilt c.1530; escaped Great Fire; restored several times in 19th and 20th centuries; damaged by IRA bomb 1992

Dedicated to the Apostle, this church stands in the heart of the City's insurance sector. The plain stone exterior is literally in the shadow of the Swiss Re 'gherkin' towering above it and the Lloyd's Underwriting Centre opposite. This Perpendicular Gothic building is chiefly notable for being one of the few complete late medieval churches left in the City, the structure dating mainly from 1520-32 and funded largely by Lord Mayor Sir Stephen Jennings. 'Undershaft' refers to the massive maypole (or 'shaft') that once stood beside the church, probably taller than the tower. The maypole was important in the May Day festival and at other times was possibly stored under the eaves of local houses in nearby Shaft Alley, hence the name. However the maypole was taken down following the infamous 'Evil May Day' of 1517 when City apprentices went on the rampage to express their opposition to the influx of foreign workers. Many apprentices were punished and Shakespeare is believed to have written scenes depicting the riot in the unstaged play 'Sir Thomas More'. Later the maypole, as with many pre-Reformation symbols, was denounced as a 'heathen idol' by the curate of nearby St Katherine Cree in 1549 and soon after chopped up and burnt.

If you look up from the base of the 15th-century tower you will see the distinctive turret and four pinnacles at the top, which were added in 1883. Stop to look at the door knocker, once used by those seeking the ancient right of sanctuary inside. The Gothic interior consists of a nave and north and south aisles and is particularly noted for the quality of its 17th-century carvings. The flat wooden roof over the nave is modern but incorporates original late medieval bosses, including Henry VIII's rose. Sadly the 17th-century west window depicting the English monarchs was destroyed in the 1992 IRA bombing – the current window is a replacement.

Looking up high to the nave arcades you can see a unique series of paintings just below the windows depicting the life of Christ, painted by Robert Brown c.1726. On the west wall of the south aisle is a memorial to Hans Holbein the Younger (d.1543), painter to the court of Henry VIII, who lived in the parish just before he died of the plague. On the north-east wall you will find a 1539 brass commemorating Sheriff of London Nicholas Leveson, his wife Dionysia, and their 18 children. Dionysia was the daughter of Sir Thomas Bodley, founder of the Bodleian Library in Oxford. The beautiful font (c.1634) just under the west window was made by Nicholas Stone, master mason to James I and Charles I and the wooden font cover is said to be the work of Grinling Gibbons. John Stow (1525-1605), the first person to accurately document the City and its churches in his 'Survey of London' (1598), was buried here. His alabaster memorial dating from 1605 stands on the north-east corner of the north aisle, and depicts Stow at his desk holding a real quill pen (see opposite). The pen is renewed every three years by the Lord Mayor during a special service and until recently the old pen and a copy of Stow's book were presented as a prize to the child who wrote the best essay on London. Stow had to resort to obtaining a begging licence from James I in order to fund his work, however the result is an incredibly important record of Elizabethan London. There is another imposing memorial in the chancel to Sir Thomas Offley (d.1582). The splendid Renatus Harris organ dates from 1696. The church is not generally open to the public and is used mainly for Bible study groups.

St Mary Axe, EC3; Nearest transport Bank LU; Open by arrangement only (telephone St Helen's, 020 7283 2231)

St Andrew Undershaft

St Andrew by the Wardrobe

5. St Andrew by the Wardrobe

First recorded c.1170; destroyed in the Great Fire; rebuilt by Wren but destroyed in Blitz; reopened 1961

Dedicated to the Apostle, St Andrew's stands on busy Queen Victoria Street and opposite Blackfriars Station. The red brick exterior is more attractive than you might expect given this was Wren's cheapest (and last) parish church. St Andrew's was originally called St Andrea de Castello, a reference to Baynard's Castle that once stood nearby. Baynard was a Norman who arrived with William the Conqueror and his castle was later used by the English monarchy, including Henry VIII who used it to provide accommodation for his wives. 'Wardrobe' refers to church's location beside the King's Great Wardrobe, where royal costumes and belongings were kept from 1361 until being moved after the Great Fire. Despite these royal connections, this parish was nevertheless once one of the poorest in the City. After St Andrew's was destroyed in the Great Fire of 1666 the subsequent rebuilding by Wren (1685-94) was restricted to funds derived from the coal tax levied to help the post-Fire reconstruction. Wren's church was once hemmed in by surrounding buildings, however the construction of Queen Victoria Street in 1871 exposed the church and removed its extensive churchyard.

Shakespeare lived in this parish, owning a house in Ireland Yard nearby. The playwright worked for around 15 years at the Blackfriars theatre he jointly owned and which his company, the King's Men, continued to use after his death right up until the theatre was closed in 1642 during the English Civil War. The site of the theatre is remembered by Playhouse Yard close to the church. Shakespeare more than likely visited the Wardrobe to organise the collection of cloth and materials for his Court productions and it is known his troupe was given scarlet woollen cloth from the Wardrobe for its part in James I's flamboyant coronation procession that started from the Tower and ended at Westminster. Inside the church on the western gallery is a modern oak and lime wood

33

memorial to Shakespeare, although given his family's suspected Roman Catholic connections it is uncertain if he was ever a regular member of the congregation. Beside the monument to Shakespeare is a similar one to his once famous musical contemporary John Dowland (d.1626). Dowland was buried in St Ann, Blackfriars, a church that was destroyed in 1666 and whose parish was then merged with that of St Andrew's. The interior of St Andrew's is not of great historical interest, being gutted during the Blitz leaving only the walls and tower. It was restored by Marshall Sisson using Wren's original plans and re-opened in 1961. The font and restored pulpit came from the 'lost' City church of St Matthew Friday Street. There is also a memorial window on the west end to MP and author Ivor Bulmer-Thomas, who was once a churchwarden here. The banners hanging down from the gallery over the nave signify St Andrew's connections with various City Livery companies, including the Mercers' and the Blacksmiths' Companies. The church also contains a wooden figure of St Anne holding the Virgin and Child, probably North Italian (c.1500). *The Times* used to be printed nearby and until the '70s the paper contained the statement 'printed and published in the parish of St Andrew-by-the-Wardrobe'.

Queen Victoria Street, EC4; Nearest transport Blackfriars LU/Rail; Open Mon-Fri 10am-4pm

6. St Anne and St Agnes

First mentioned 1150; original church burnt down and rebuilt c.1548; destroyed in Great Fire and rebuilt by Wren; damaged in Blitz, reopened 1966

St Anne and St Agnes is a pretty Wren church located on the north side of Gresham Street, and the City's only remaining Lutheran place of worship. St Anne was the mother of the Virgin Mary, whilst St Agnes was an obscure virgin martyr who died aged 13 at the hands of the Romans in 304 AD. This double dedication is unique, although the reason behind it remains unclear. It is known that the cult of the Virgin Mary was strong in medieval times, arousing great interest in her parents, although this particular dedication is unusual as Luther himself strongly discouraged the cult. Confusingly, the original church was known either as St Anne or St Agnes during the medieval period. It was not until the 15th century that both saints were incorporated into the official name. The church was rebuilt after destruction by a fire in 1548. It was destroyed again during the Great Fire and rebuilt by Wren (1677-87), although his eminent assistant Robert Hooke is thought to have made a substantial contribution to the design and was recorded as visiting the site several times. Incorporating part of the 14th-century tower, Wren's church was largely of brick and was later renovated and altered a number of times during the 19th century. Until the Second World War the church was only just visible through a gap in the buildings of Gresham Street, however the area was flattened during the Blitz and the gutted church restored carefully by Braddock and Martin-Smith (1963-66).

Standing on the site of the former churchyard – now one of the City churches' most pleasant gardens – the red brick exterior is rather nondescript. If you look up at the tower you can see the large 'A' that tops the weather vane. The small interior is far more appealing with its dark wooden furnishings and large clear glass windows – characteristic of Wren. After the Blitz the church was carefully restored to Wren's design and contains many furnishings from 'lost' City churches. These include the early 18th-century paintings of Moses and Aaron on either side of the altar and originally from St Michael Wood Street. The central dome is supported by four handsome Corinthian columns, two of which contain heraldic representations of the lion and unicorn, emblems of England and Scotland and a reminder of the Crown's supremacy within the Church of England. The Royal Arms of Charles II on the west wall are one of the best examples in England.

John Wesley, founder of Methodism (d.1791), twice preached here, including during the period of his famous 'conversion' in 1738. Notable parishioners included poet John Milton and John Bunyan, author of *The Pilgrim's Progress*. Like some of its parishioners the church has fallen foul of authority – in 1649 the vicar was beheaded for protesting the execution of Charles I. High up on the south wall are busts of Sir James Drax (d.1662) and his son John (d.1682), originally from St John Zachary which was united with this parish in 1670. The site of this lost church is marked by a sign nearby to the east along Gresham Street. The Drax family were pioneers in the establishment of the sugar industry (and slavery) in Barbados, and Drax Hall Plantation in St George, Barbados is the oldest surviving Jacobean mansion in the western hemisphere.

After the Second World War the building was given over to the Lutheran Church who paid for the excellent restoration and it was reconsecrated on St George's Day 1966. The church is today the pre-eminent place for Lutheran worship in London although it was not the first Lutheran church to be founded in the City - German artisans involved in the reconstruction of the City after the Great Fire founded an earlier church c.1669 near Mansion House. There are regular services in many languages, particularly Estonian, Latvian and Swahili. The church also has excellent acoustics and is known for the quality of its regular concerts, particularly the Bach Vespers. The Lutheran Church has always had a very strong musical tradition and many Lutheran composers wrote for their churches including Bach and Mendelssohn. The visitor during a lunchtime concert is likely to be supplied with coffee and enjoy an organ recital played to a large audience, many of whom will probably be eating their sandwiches and enjoying the informal atmosphere – very different from an Anglican church.

Gresham Street, EC2; Nearest transport St Paul's LU; Open Mon-Fri 10am-6pm, Sun 10am-8pm

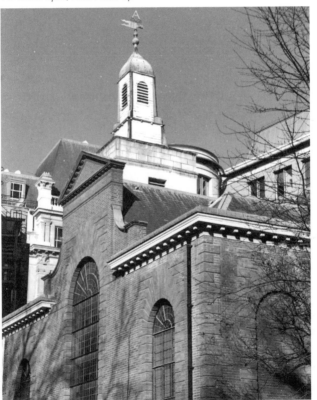

St Anne and St Agnes

St Bartholomew the Great

7. St Bartholomew the Great

Founded 12th century, post-Reformation church reduced in size; major alterations 16th-17th century, escaped Great Fire, restored late 19th century by Aston Webb; escaped Blitz

St Bartholomew's is one of the great City churches and a rare legacy of the medieval priories that dominated pre-Reformation London. Hidden behind a gatehouse, St Bartholomew's has one of the finest Norman interiors in the capital, often described as having a cathedral like quality. The church was founded in 1123 by Rahere, courtier and minstrel to Henry I. Taken ill in Rome, Rahere had a vision in which St Bartholomew, the Apostle martyred in India, told him to build a church at 'smoothfield', or Smithfield as it is called today. The cult of St Bartholomew was strong in medieval times, particularly after King Cnut's wife presented the Archbishop of Canterbury with the relic of the saint's arm.

In gratitude for his miraculous recovery, Rahere founded an Augustinian priory on this site which contained a church and hospital for the poor. The current church, as imposing as it is today, is but a shadow of Rahere's building. To get a better sense of the original size, stand at the gateway and imagine the stone arch (sitting under a Tudor timber structure) forming the entrance to the south aisle that led along the path up to the church. Rahere's priory was situated in what was once (and has recently become again) one of London's most vibrant areas. It held the rights to the famous 'Cloth Fair' (or 'Bartholomew Fair') held annually for three days beginning on St Bartholomew's Day (24 August), and remembered today in the street called Cloth Fair that runs alongside the church. The houses at 41–42 Cloth Fair are possibly the oldest in London, dating from c.1600, and protected from the Great Fire by virtue of being enclosed by the old priory wall. The Saint's Day also attracted the sick, drawn to the church's reputation for having curative powers. The Fair was originally a meeting place for cloth merchants, but developed into a famous pleasure festival that survived until 1855 when the Victorian authorities could no longer tolerate its excesses.

Medieval jousting tournaments and public executions took place in Smithfield and near the gatehouse. You can see memorials both to Protestant martyrs burnt at the stake, and Scotland's 'Braveheart' Sir William Wallace (d.1305) who was hung, drawn and quartered here. Later, in the 17th century a cattle market was established and today Smithfield remains a major London meat market.

The priory building was surrendered to Henry VIII in 1539 during the Dissolution of the Monasteries. The nave was destroyed, but the choir and transepts of the priory church were allowed to continue as a parish church and over the following centuries much renovation was carried out. The brick tower was added in the 1620s, whilst much of the current shape of the church was developed during a major restoration in the 1890s by Aston Webb. Henry VIII also permitted Rahere's priory hospital to reopen and today the adjacent St Bartholomew's is the oldest hospital in London. Over the centuries parts of the original church building were used for commercial purposes, including a school, a smithy, and a printing works. The priory cloister, the eastern walk of which you can see to the right of the entrance, was even used as a horse stable. These various uses have contributed to the blackened appearance of the stonework, although in Norman times the interior was probably brightly painted. Benjamin Franklin (1706-1790), American statesman and scientist, worked in 1725 for a printer located within the Lady Chapel behind the altar. William Hogarth (1697-1764), English artist, was christened here in 1697 and Sir Walter Mildmay, founder of Emmanuel College Cambridge, was buried here in 1589. His tomb can be seen on the south aisle. Rahere's tomb of 1405 lies just to the left of the altar and depicts him clad in the black Augustinian habit. If you look up at the south side of the gallery you will see the oriel window looking down over Rahere's tomb. Built by Prior Bolton, perhaps to enable him to keep an eye on gifts being left on the tomb, the window dates from c.1520. Bolton's 'rebus' or heraldic emblem can be seen just below the window. The church's pre-Reformation five bells are the oldest complete ring in London, each one named after a saint – Anne, John, Peter, Katherine and, of course, Bartholomew. The church has regular traditional services throughout the week principally serving the local Barbican population. If you are ever in the City on the day of the Lord Mayor's Show be sure to visit the church's excellent annual bazaar afterwards. The church has also been used in several films and television productions, including *Shakespeare in Love*, *Four Weddings and a Funeral* and *Spooks*.

West Smithfield, EC1; Nearest transport Barbican and Farringdon LU/Rail, St Paul's LU; Open Tues-Fri 8.30am-5pm (4pm in winter), Sat 10.30am-1.30pm, Sun 8am-1pm and 2pm-8pm

St Bartholomew the Great

St Bartholomew the Less

8. St Bartholomew the Less

First recorded 12th century; rebuilt by George Dance the Younger 1793, rebuilt 1823-25; gutted in Blitz, reopened 1951

This small church is one of the least well known of all the City churches, tucked away inside the grounds of St Bartholomew's (London's oldest hospital). When walking through the hospital gatehouse off Smithfield look up to see a statue of Henry VIII, the only such statue in London, and then turn almost immediately left. The hospital was founded in 1123 by Rahere (see St Bartholomew the Great for more information) and on this site was originally a hospital chapel dating from around 1190. There was little the hospital could do for Wat Tyler, leader of the Peasant's Revolt against the introduction of a poll tax in the 14th century. In 1381 Tyler met a young King Richard II outside the Hospital gates and was stabbed by Lord Mayor William Walworth. After some disorder, Walworth returned to find Tyler's body and a contemporary chronicle recorded that 'it was told him that [Tyler] had been carried by some of the commons to the hospital for poor folks by St Bartholomew's, and was put to bed in the chamber of the master of hospital. In the Mayor went thither and found him and had him carried out to the middle of Smithfield, in presence of his fellows, and there beheaded. And thus ended his wretched life'. Later, when Henry VIII shut down St Bartholomew's Priory during the Dissolution, he allowed the hospital to remain open and it was refounded by Royal Charter c. 1547. The chapel, the only one of a number in the original hospital to survive, was converted into a parish church and known as 'the Less' to distinguish it from its better known sister church nearby.

The church resides over a parish bounded by the walls of the hospital itself, the only such hospital parish in existence. It therefore has close connections with those who have worked at the hospital over the centuries and their patients. In the 18th century the church structure fell into disrepair and was rebuilt in 1789-91 by George Dance the Younger whose rectangular building incorporated a rather unusual octagonal interior. However the structure was not very sturdy and had to be rebuilt again in 1823-25 by Thomas Hardwick. He retained Dance's original design and much of the tower and vestry survive from the earlier 15th-century hospital chapel. The modest interior displays much restoration work carried out by both the Victorians and the post-war architects following Blitz damage. However, it also retains many interesting historical monuments to physicians, surgeons and nurses from the 17th century onwards, making it worth a visit. Inigo Jones, who restored St Paul's shortly before it was destroyed in the Great Fire, was christened here in 1573. There is a memorial to Robert Balthrope, Queen Elizabeth I's sergeant surgeon (d. 1591) and one to Lady Anne Bodley (d.1611). Her husband, Sir Thomas Bodley, founded the Bodleian Library at Oxford and their house stood inside the hospital precincts. Sir Thomas was an innovator and set up an agreement with the Stationers' Company in London by which one copy of every book printed in England would be sent for deposit at the Library. The modern stained glass on the west side depicts St Bartholomew, Rahere, and the physician St Luke. Two of the four bells originate from the 15th century and are held within a medieval bell frame that is one of the oldest in London. Today, given the many religions of those attending the hospital, there are a variety of services. The atmosphere is certainly more relaxed than a few centuries ago when services were obligatory for nursing staff, with patients also expected to attend unless they were too ill. On my last visit a member of the Augustinian Order was giving a Roman Catholic service – fitting given that the hospital was founded by Rahere as part of the Augustinian priory.

St Bartholomew's Hospital, EC1; Nearest transport Barbican and Farringdon LU/Rail, St Paul's LU; Open daily 7am-8pm or later

St Bartholomew the Less

St Benet Paul's Wharf

9. St Benet Paul's Wharf

First recorded early 12th century; destroyed in Great Fire, rebuilt by Wren

Dedicated to the 6th century St Benedict who founded the original monastic code, St Benet's is not a particularly accessible church. It is rarely open to the public and stands rather isolated beside the fast traffic of Queen Victoria Street high above. This is a shame as this is in fact one of the most attractive Wren churches, with its elegant but simple exterior of red and blue chequered brickwork and Portland stone. It is also unique in the City for being the 'Welsh' church, holding services in the Welsh native tongue for over 100 years although today it serves an ever dwindling congregation. Originally known as St Benedict's by the Thames, St Benet's lies south of St Paul's, and once stood beside the wharf or quay where materials were offloaded for use in the construction of Wren's great cathedral. Today the proximity of the Thames is no longer so apparent since the subsequent widening of the river embankment over the following centuries. Although destroyed in the Great Fire, the church is largely unaltered since being rebuilt by Wren between 1678-84 in what is regarded as a Dutch style, although there is evidence the design was principally by Wren's assistant Robert Hooke.

Fortunate to have survived the Blitz, this modestly sized building is worth visiting simply because it is arguably the least spoilt of all Wren's remaining City churches with most of its 17th-century furnishings still intact. Worth seeing is the original poor box and the magnificent Flemish oak communion table given to the church in 1686. The church also retains 17th-century galleries supported by Corinthian columns – such galleries used to be common throughout the City churches of Wren's time, but today they are very rare. A fine example of the Stuart royal arms of Charles II is to be found over the door case of the tower as you enter. Just above this is a bricked-up entrance that once led to a small gallery used, it is said, by Charles II to attend services in privacy. The colourful shields up on the north gallery are evidence of the church's long-standing connection with the nearby College of Arms, the centre for heraldry in the UK. Over the centuries those seeking to prove their gentlemanly credentials had first to convince The College's Royal Heralds. The College retains the notes made by the sceptical Herald who quizzed William Shakespeare and his father John when they applied (perhaps in person) for a family coat of arms. The church has been the chapel and burial place of the College since 1555.

The church contains a monument to England's first great architect, Inigo Jones (1573-1652). Jones designed Banqueting Hall at Whitehall, restored 'old' St Paul's and planned the layout of Covent Garden. He was buried in the old church in 1652. Henry Fielding (1707-54), author of Tom Jones and Amelia, married his first wife's former maid here in 1747. Elias Ashmole (1617-92), antiquarian, was married in the old church in 1638. Later his collection was given to Oxford University and is now housed in the famous Ashmolean Museum. The church also contains a splendid white marble bust of Sir Robert Wyseman (d.1684). Sir Robert was Dean of the Court of Arches, the Archbishop of Canterbury's chief ecclesiastical court, once held at St Mary le Bow. St Benet's has another Shakespearean connection, being possibly referred to in *Twelfth Night* in the clown's line 'the bells of St Bennet, sir may put you in mind; one, two, three'. The church was one of 19 City churches due for demolition in 1877, however an Order in Council signed by Queen Victoria removed St Benet's from the list. It was given to the Welsh Episcopalian Church, temporarily homeless after their church at St Etheldreda, Ely Place had been put up for auction. St Benet's remains the Welsh church within the Church of England London Diocese.

Paul's Wharf, Queen Victoria Street, EC4; Nearest transport Blackfriars LU/Rail; Open 1st Monday in month 11am-3.30pm or by arrangement (tel 020 7489 8754)

10. St Botolph without Aldersgate

Saxon origins likely, first mentioned early 12th century; medieval church largely escaped Great Fire; rebuilt c.1791, further work 1831; restored 1990s

St Botolph's is a tranquil, seldom visited church, whose unusual stuccoed olive green frontage on busy Aldersgate Street is not obviously that of a church at all. It is named after the 7th-century Saxon Abbot Botolph, popular medieval patron saint of travellers, and is one of three surviving City churches with a similar dedication. The four original St Botolph's were each situated beside one of the old City gates through which all travellers had to pass – they would often stop at these churches to seek a blessing from the saint for a new journey or safe arrival. This church stood outside (or 'without') Aldersgate, a gate house in the old Roman wall that once stood opposite number 62 in this street. The medieval church was rebuilt in the early 17th century and its location outside the City wall saved St Botolph's from the worst ravages of the Great Fire that raged within. Whilst it suffered only minor damage it was later rebuilt in 1789-91 by Nathaniel Wright, surveyor to the City. The classical green façade with a Venetian window facing onto Aldersgate Street was added c.1831 after the church had to be shortened to allow for the widening of the road. The rest of the exterior is in a rather drab red brick, overshadowed by neighbouring office blocks.

The interior, with its elaborate barrel-vaulted roof and bell turret, is a graceful example of late Georgian church building and described by Pevsner as having 'extreme elegance'. It is similar in style to George Dance the Younger's design at All Hallows London Wall and Wright is thought to have been influenced by this earlier building. The plaster ceiling is particularly lavish, although the overall combination of Georgian design mixed with sometimes heavy-handed later additions (such as the stained glass, pews and tiled flooring) is not wholly successful. The simple yet impressive late 18th-century pulpit stands balanced on a carved palm and is made from imported tulip wood from Carolina. It is said to have been made by master furniture maker Thomas Chippendale who lived and worked nearby. The walls are crowded with monuments largely from the earlier church, most notably Lady Anne Packington's Gothic altar tomb of 1563 situated on the south-east corner. There is also a white marble cartouche complete with cherub, skulls and hourglass remembering Christopher Tamworth (d.1624) and his wife (d.1637). The south wall contains a fine monument to Sir John Micklethwaite (d.1682), thought to be a rare example of a stone carving in a City church by Grinling Gibbons. Of particular merit is the east window 'transparency' from 1788 depicting the 'Agony in the Garden' by James Pearson. The window is beautifully illuminated when the light shines through its painted glass at certain times during the day, although the post-Blitz replacement flanking windows slightly reduce the overall impact. The church also contains some original wooden galleries with box pews upstairs, now a rare feature in the City churches. The stained glass windows on the north ground floor were presented by the congregation in memory of other parishioners. The one nearest the entrance depicts Captain Matthew Webb (d. 1883), the first person to swim across the English Channel. He died whilst attempting to swim the Niagra River.

At the East end is a memorial book recording the names of nearly 1800 members of the Post Office Rifles who died in action during the Great War, evidence of St Botolph's connections with the London General Post Office that was once situated nearby. This proximity resulted in the former churchyard behind the church becoming known as 'Postman's Park' – this delightful space is definitely worth a visit even if St Botolph's is rarely open to visitors. With headstones stacked up against each other along the walls, the park contains the famous Watts' Cloister, built by the Victorian artist GF Watts in commemoration of unsung heroes. The Victorian phrasing in each glazed tile memorial at first seems unintentionally amusing, for example Sarah Smith who died 'whilst attempting in her inflammable dress to extinguish flames'. they are, however, a poignant reminder of London's long-forgotten 'have a go' heroes. One plaque remembers Alice Ayers who died saving three children. Her name was assumed by the character of Jane in Patrick Marber's award-winning play 'Closer'.

Aldersgate Street, EC1; Nearest transport St Paul's LU; Rarely open, although lunchtime services held Tuesday and Thursday

St Botolph without Aldersgate

St Botolph without Aldgate

11. St Botolph without Aldgate

Saxon origins likely; first mentioned 1125; rebuilt early 16th century; escaped Great Fire; rebuilt by George Dance the Elder 18th century; renovated 19th century

As with the other two surviving City churches that have a similar dedication to the Saxon patron saint of travellers, St Botolph's was once situated beside a City gate, in this case Ald Gate on the eastern edge of the City. Today, this imposing church stands as if marooned on a concrete island within a busy road network on the edge of the City, its plain brick exterior and Portland stone tower facing south onto Aldgate High Street. A church has existed here for possibly one thousand years – few other City churches have such an ancient history. St Botolph's was once owned by the Knighten Guild, an elite group of warriors founded by the Saxon King Edgar. Later, in the 12th century, it was given to the Priory of the Holy Trinity, one of the richest monasteries in England. It was rebuilt by the Priory but during the Dissolution of the Monasteries in the 1530s fell into the hands of Henry VIII.

Although the church survived the Great Fire, it became unsafe and was eventually pulled down. It was rebuilt in 1741-44 by George Dance the Elder, one of London's most eminent architects, however to the casual observer it could be mistaken for a Wren design. During the reconstruction the well preserved body of a boy in a standing position was discovered in the vaults and attracted a paying crowd of visitors. In the late 19th century JF Bentley, famous architect of the Roman Catholic Westminster Cathedral, completely refurbished the largely empty and undistinguished church. He lowered the galleries and installed balustrades and reworked the ceiling and underside of the galleries with dramatic plasterwork incorporating angels and shields. During this era the church was known as the 'Prostitutes' church' because of its vicinity to a Victorian red-light district – Catherine Eddowes, a victim of the Jack the Ripper, was seen drunk near St Botolph's just before her murder in September 1888. During the Second World War the church survived the Blitz but only just – a bomb landed on the roof without exploding. It was later restored after a fire in the 1960s. One of the first things the visitor notices upon entering the church today is how well lit the large galleried interior is, thanks to the well spaced Venetian windows on three sides. Above the entrance is a fine Renatus Harris organ dating from 1676, with a 18th-century case by John Byfield. In the baptistery just inside the main entrance is a monument to Lord Darcy and Sir Nicholas Carew. Both were beheaded on Tower Hill in the 1530s by Henry VIII for their treasonable activities and buried in the church. Nearby there is also an arresting and colourful monument from 1623 to one time master of the Merchant Taylors Company, Robert Dow – his hands resting ominously upon a skull.

Daniel Defoe (1660-1731), author of Robinson Crusoe, was married here in 1683. In his account of the Great Plague, Defoe described how the churchyard plague pits were filled with bodies of more than 5,000 people in just four months. Jeremy Bentham, the utilitarian philosopher, was christened here in 1748. Edmund Spenser (1552-99), the poet who penned The Faerie Queene, was born in this parish. A rather macabre point of historical interest is a mummified head which was kept on show to visitors until being re-buried in 1968 in the foundations of the new vestry. The head is reputed to have belonged to Lady Jane Grey's father, the Duke of Suffolk, who was beheaded in the Tower in 1554. Today the church is at the forefront of the City churches attempts to help the local poor. The crypt was opened by George Appleton, later Archbishop of Perth, as a base for homeless men in the 1960s. The poet John Betjeman, a keen scholar of the City churches, described the church as 'more a mission to the East End than a City church'. A statement that I suspect would not be unappreciated by the current rector.

Aldgate EC3; Nearest transport Aldgate LU;
Open Mon-Fri 9.30am-3pm

St Botolph without Aldgate

A MEMORIALL ERECTED BY THE RIGHTE WORP: THE COMPANY OF MARCHANTAILO
ROBERT DOW ESQ. CITIZEN & MARCHANTAILO OF LONDON & MASTER OF THE
COMPANY & ONE OF THE CVSTOMERS IN THE PORT OF LONDON WHO GAVE IN
TYME 352 8.10 8.8 D. TO PERFORME DIVERS CHARITABLE DEEDS FOR EVER TO DIV
ETHREN OF THE SAME COMPANY & OTHER VSES FOR THE SAID COMPANY, VIZ
SPITALL, TO S T. SEPVLCHRES PARISHE TO THE TWO COMPTERS, TO LVDGAT
WGATE TO THE POORE OF THIS PARISH TO S T. JOHN BAPTIST COLLEDGE
RD, AND TO QVEENE ELIZABETHS HOSPITALL AT BRISTOLL.

S 8.10.8. TO Y COMPANY   320 L.00.00   TO CHRIST HOSPITALL,   050.00,00,TO
00,00. TO S T. JOHNS COLL IN OXON,   100 L.00.00   TO THE CITY OF B

LIVED VERTVOVSLY ALL HIS LIFE TYME & DYED IN Y TRVE FAITH OF OVR
ECOND DAY OF MAY AN. DM 1612 . BEING FVLL OF DAIES AT THE AGE O

St Botolph without Bishopsgate

12. St Botolph without Bishopsgate

Saxon origins; first recorded late 12th century; 16th century building survived Great Fire but re-built 18th century by James Gold; many restorations since including after IRA bombs 1992/93; reopened 1997

This is one of three surviving City churches dedicated to St Botolph, the popular medieval patron saint of travellers. St Botolph's was situated near Bishop's Gate, which itself stood opposite Camomile Street. It is thought there has been a place of worship here since Saxon times and possibly even earlier. Whilst the medieval church survived the Great Fire, it was rebuilt by James Gold between 1725-28 under the supervision of his son-in-law, and pre-eminent City architect of the day, George Dance the Elder. It was during this time that Gold discovered the foundations of a much earlier Saxon church. The current grand, mostly red brick church reflects the wealth of what was once one of the City's 'richest livings'. Many prosperous and prominent Londoners, including Shakespeare, lived on Bishopsgate until it succumbed to office blocks in the 20th Century. Before you enter, stop to look at the 19th-century red-brick former charity school building on the west side. Unfortunately its pretty exterior statues of children (c.1820), made out of Coade stone, are being restored following vandalism.

Bishopsgate is probably the busiest part of the City, so it is unsurprising that St Botolph's pleasant garden is often crowded – its grounds also host netball games for office workers and contains the only public tennis court in the City. When the garden was opened in 1863 its conversion from the former churchyard caused great controversy – surprising given the later demolition of so many Wren churches by the Victorians. The church also once stood beside the Priory of Bethlehem, shut down by Henry VIII in 1535, and later converted into a lunatic hospital. The hospital's nickname 'Bedlam' passed into the English language as meaning a 'madhouse' or 'scene of uproar'.

St Botolph's is unique in the City for having its tower on the east side, and chancel underneath. The galleried interior with its giant Corinthian columns is very fine although somewhat dark, despite the unusual early 19th-century glass dome above the nave. Whilst it contains some Georgian fittings – notably the font, pulpit and John Byfield organ (c.1764) – the Victorians are responsible for much of the rest, including the screens, stained glass, paintings and choir stalls. Below the galleries you can see inscribed the names of the church's rectors since 1323, including the eminent Victorian social reformer William Rogers who founded the nearby Bishopsgate Institute. On the west end there is a poignant modern memorial icon by Michael Coles to those haemophiliacs who have died through contaminated blood treatment and featuring St Luke the physician.

The church has many historical connections. In the early 14th century Templar knights, crusaders and guardians of the Holy Land, were subject to an inquisition here on charges of corruption. Later, parishioner and Lord Mayor Sir William Allen rebuilt the medieval church in 1571 at his own expense. Edward Alleyn (1566-1626), famous tragic actor and theatre manager, friend of Shakespeare and founder of Dulwich College, was baptised here, as was the poet John Keats (1795-1821). Ben Jonson (1573-1637), dramatist and poet, buried a son in the old church. There is also a tablet near the gallery stairs (ask to see) in memory of eminent ambassador Sir Paul Pinder (d.1650). The grand façade of his Bishopsgate house is preserved today in the Victoria and Albert Museum. Sadly, whilst the church largely survived the Blitz (it was restored 1947-8), it sustained severe damage by both IRA bombs of 1992 and 1993 and was not reopened until 1997. Today it is a quiet church, often with more people in the garden than inside. It does, however, hold regular services, hosts a youth club and hire out the hall for various activities.

Bishopsgate EC1; Nearest transport Liverpool Street LU/Rail; Open Mon-Fri 8am-5.30pm

13. St Bride's Fleet Street

Roman/Saxon origins, rebuilt by Normans; destroyed in the Great Fire; rebuilt by Wren; gutted in Blitz; reopened 1957

With the exception of St Mary le Bow, St Bride's is possibly the most famous City church, principally because of its 'wedding cake' steeple and journalistic connections. The original church was said to have been built by St Bridget (hence 'Bride') of Kildare on the site of an earlier Roman graveyard and buildings. In Kildare today can be found the remains of a church with very similar foundations to those discovered at St Bride's during the post-Blitz restoration. Bridget's feast day coincides with that of Brigit, a Pagan goddess of fertility and churches with a similar dedication can often be found symbolically near wells. Bride's well, once found in the churchyard, was said to have miraculous healing powers, the water even turning into beer on the saint's day. The 16th-century royal palace of 'Bridewell' was situated nearby, later becoming a prison of such notoriety that the name has since passed into the English language as meaning a place of detention.

The original church, probably founded amongst a fledgling Irish community, is one of the earliest known Christian places of worship in London. It was rebuilt many times over the centuries, the current building thought to be the seventh structure on the site. The medieval Norman church was used in 1205 as the location of the Curia Regis, the first court of the State, and by King John for his parliament of 1210. The Great Fire destroyed the 15th-century building and it was rebuilt by Wren (1671-78) in a style befitting the great wealth of the parish. St Bride's was Wren's most expensive, and arguably (with St Stephen Walbrook) his finest parish church. The famously elaborate steeple was only one aspect of what was then an influential design, and it is a tragedy that the Blitz destroyed the core of such a magnificent building. The steeple, with its four diminishing octagonal stages, was added in 1703 and originally stood 234 feet high. It is famous for being the inspiration for the design of the traditional wedding cake, first created by Mr Rich, a

St Bride's

pastry chef on Ludgate Hill. He made his fortune selling cakes modelled on the steeple until his death in 1811. After damage by lightning strikes in 1764 the steeple was reduced in height by 8 feet, sparking a furious row between George III and American statesman and inventor Benjamin Franklin over the apparently controversial topic of whether lightning conductors should be blunt or sharp-edged. Evidently Mr Franklin had come a long way from his origins as a lowly worker for a printing press located inside the church of St Bartholomew the Great.

This is also the 'Journalist's Church', St Bride's association with writers literally going back to the origins of the printing press itself. William Caxton printed the first book in English. After Caxton's death, in 1501 his apprentice – Wynkyn de Worde – moved his master's famous printing press from Westminster to Fleet Street in order to be nearer the wealthy ecclesiastical client base. Worde was buried in the church in 1535 but not before his press had attracted other printers and writers to the area. During the 16th and 17th centuries many writers lived in the parish, including John Milton, John Evelyn, John Dryden and Richard Lovelace (the latter being buried in the old church). Coffee houses and taverns sprung up around Fleet Street to service this new clientele and these also became the haunt of famous literary figures from Johnson and Boswell to Dickens. Legions of Fleet Street hacks worked and played in this part of town until the press largely abandoned the area during 1980s.

Diarist Samuel Pepys was a parishioner, born in nearby Axe Lane, and christened here together with his eight brothers and sisters. During the Great Plague of 1664 Pepys records bribing the grave digger to 'justle together' the bodies because of the 'fulness of the middle aisle' in order to make space for his dead brother Tom. St Bride's has some notable American connections. Near the font is a modern bust (the original was stolen) of Virginia Dare, the first child to be born in the English colony in North Carolina in 1587, whose parents were married here. Sadly, Dare was destined to perish with the rest of Sir Walter Raleigh's 'lost colony'. The parents of

Edward Wimslow (d.1655), one of the Pilgrim Fathers, were also married here. Beside the bust of Dare are two 17th-century wooden figures of children that originally stood outside a nearby charity school. Today, the interior is well lit, smart and colourful – an excellent example of a post-Blitz restoration. Excavations during the rebuilding uncovered the church's long rumoured Saxon origins – you should include a visit to the fascinating crypt (entrance just to the right as you enter the church) that houses a small museum showing evidence of the Norman and Saxon discoveries. The elegant former *Daily Telegraph* and *Daily Express* buildings opposite St Bride's on Fleet Street, now inhabited by a US merchant bank, stand as testimony to the passing of the great age of the press in this area. However the church still has many associations with the industry and owes its current structure largely to the sums contributed by the major newspapers during the post-War rebuilding. Even to this day memorial services for journalists are often held at St Bride's. The church is also well known for the quality of its professional choir.

Fleet Street, EC4; Nearest transport Blackfriars LU/Rail and Chancery Lane LU; Open Mon-Fri 8am-6pm, Sat 11am-3pm, Sun 10am-1pm, 5pm-7.30pm

St Bride's

St Clement

14. St Clement Eastcheap

Founded 11th century; destroyed by Great Fire; rebuilt by Wren; restored late 19th century by Butterfield; 1930s restoration by Comper

St Clement's is a small, unassuming church, half-hidden down Clement's Lane and dedicated to the third bishop of Rome. Clement was martyred by the Romans, who tossed him into the sea with an anchor around his neck and thus he became the patron saint of sailors. The original medieval church was first officially recorded in 1067 in a charter that confirmed grants of livings by William the Conqueror. The church has a list of rectors beginning in around 1308 when the church was known as St Clement Candlewickstrate, the latter being the old name of nearby Cannon Street. The medieval church was later rebuilt but survived only until 1666 when it was one of the first buildings to be destroyed in the Great Fire that started in nearby Pudding Lane.

Wren rebuilt the church (1683–87), earning one third of a hogshead of wine from the grateful parishioners, but it is not one of his more memorable designs. It has a stuccoed exterior with the tower on the south-west corner, although given the narrowness of the lane it is hard for the visitor to stand far enough back to get a good view. The interior is oblong and plain, yet still atmospheric. It is full of rich wood panelling and divided into a nave and south aisle under a lofty plaster ceiling.

William Butterfield carried out typically extensive Victorian renovations to the interior in 1872 and 1889, which even the church guide describes as 'drastic'. He removed the south gallery, filled Wren's clear windows with stained glass (since partially removed) and converted the box pews into benches. The striking blue and gold altar piece or reredos was disassembled by Butterfield, but then reassembled by Sir Ninian Comper in the early 1930s. Comper has been described as the greatest church furnisher since Wren and was involved in the restoration of scores of churches throughout England. The organ, restored in the 1930s to its original position above the door, was made by Renatus Harris. Edward Purcell, son of composer Henry, was once church organist here. Prime Minister William Gladstone was a great admirer of this church, bringing his grandchildren to see the font cover then on display. The church is best known for being the church referred to in the line 'Oranges and Lemons, Say the bells of St Clement's' from the famous nursery rhyme – although St Clement Danes in Aldwych is a rival for this claim. However it is a historical fact that Spanish oranges were brought onshore from a nearby Thames quay – so my vote goes with the City rather than the West End. The origins of the rhyme are obscure but it was first thought to have been printed in the 1744 book *Tommy Thumb's Pretty Song Book*. Today the church, whose parish has produced 13 Lord Mayors, is rather quiet and empty. It does, however, attract discerning City workers and passers-by to its regular second-hand book stall and hosts medieval drama in the form of mystery plays performed by *The Players of St Peter*.

Clement's Lane, EC4; Nearest transport Monument LU;
Open Mon-Fri 8.30am-5.30pm

IF YOU WOULD LIKE TO MAKE A DONATION TO THE COST OF CANDLES, PLEASE PLACE YOUR DONATION IN THE LARGE BOX AT THE BACK OF THE CHURCH

St Clement

St Dunstan in the West

15. St Dunstan in the West

First mentioned c.1170; survived Great Fire, demolished and rebuilt 1830-33 by John Shaw (Senior and Junior)

This church is dedicated to the Saxon Archbishop of Canterbury and Benedictine monk. It lies, as its name suggests, on the western edge of the City facing onto Fleet Street. The Victorian Neo-Gothic façade of Ketton stone is a tall and imposing sight even from some distance away down Fleet Street, whilst the octagonal interior is unique and richly atmospheric. In medieval times the right of appointing the rector here lay with Westminster Abbey, before passing to the Crown and then Alnwick Abbey, in Northumberland, right up until the Dissolution of the Monasteries in the 1530s. During the Great Fire the Dean of Westminster and his scholars from Westminster School helped save the church with their fire fighting efforts, aided by a miraculous change of direction in the wind. However, by the early 19th century the building was in a sorry state and when Fleet Street was widened in 1830 St Dunstan's was demolished. The current church was rebuilt by John Shaw and his identically named son between 1831-33 in an early Gothic revivalist design. The clock is by Thomas Harris and dates from 1671. The giants who strike a bell every 15 minutes are possibly Gog and Magog, the traditional guardians of the City of London, which have been represented in the Lord Mayor's Show since the reign of Henry V. The clock was added to the old church in thanksgiving for its rescue from the Great Fire and was possibly the first clock in London to have minutes marked on the dial. It was a famous landmark for Londoners and mentioned in many literary works such as Dickens' *Barnaby Rudge* and *David Copperfield* and Oliver Goldsmith's *Vicar of Wakefield*. There was uproar when the clock was removed for restoration in the 1830s and never returned. It remained in private hands until Lord Rothermere, the famous Fleet Street newspaper proprietor, finally reunited the clock with St Dunstan's in 1935. Underneath the clock is a memorial from 1930 to Lord Northcliffe, founder of *The Daily Mail*, the obelisk of which

69

was designed by Lutyens. Before going inside the church, look up at the statue (c.1586) of Queen Elizabeth I above the vestry porch. Until 1760 it stood on Lud Gate, the main western gateway into the City. It is thought to be the oldest public statue of a English monarch and even has its own private maintenance fund ($\pounds$700) donated in 1928. The vestry porch also contains weathered statues of King Lud and his two sons, also from Lud Gate.

As you enter the octagonal interior the first thing that strikes the visitor is the remarkable Christian Orthodox screen (or iconostasis) to the left of the altar which came from Romania in 1966. This is a hint that St Dunstan's hosts one of the most exotic Christian congregations in the City. The screen is over 100 years old and was originally created for the Monastery of Antim in Bucharest. The numerous side chapels are indicative of the services that take place here for various Christian faiths, including Romanian Orthodox, Lutheran, Armenian, Coptic and Nestorian. The origin of such links date from a trip made to Romania by Archbishop Michael Ramsay in 1965.

Poet John Donne was rector here in 1624-31 and Pepys would occasionally attend a sermon, noting in his diary that during one he 'stood by a pretty, modest maid whom I did labour to take by the hand and the body, but she would not, but got further and further from me'. There are numerous interesting monuments taken from the old church, including a tablet at the south end to 'ye famed swordsman' Alexander Layton (1679). At the west end is a perhaps unique dedication to 'the honest solicitor' Hobson Judkin (d.1812), the memorial being erected by his grateful clients. The four windows behind the 17th-century altar were donated by the Hoare banking family whose premises are nearby. The windows depict Archbishop Lanfranc, St Dunstan, St Anselm and also Archbishop Langton and King John at the signing of the Magna Carta. At the south end is a poignant and unusually naturalistic bust of Edward James Auriol, who drowned in 1847. He is depicted as if lying asleep with hand on heart. William Tyndale (1494-1536), who translated the New Testament into English, was once briefly a preacher here, and George Calvert was buried in the old church in 1632 – as the first Lord Baltimore he gave his name to the American city. St Dunstan's has another American connection as two ancestors of George Washington were baptised in the old church in the 1620s. The publishing industry originated on Fleet Street and the old churchyard became a centre for the book trade – books were printed here with the inscription 'Under St Dunstan's Church Fleet Street'. Isaac Walton's book *The Compleat Angler* was published here, as was John Milton's *Paradise Lost* (for which the great poet received the miserly advance of five pounds).

Fleet Street, EC4; Nearest transport Temple or Chancery Lane LU; Open every Tuesday 11am-3pm

16. The Dutch Church, Austin Friars

Founded 13th century and rebuilt 14th century; escaped Great Fire and restored 19th century; destroyed in Blitz, reopened 1954

The Dutch Church has the most modern design of any of the City churches restored after the Blitz, its rather austere Portland stone exterior dating from the rebuilding work of 1950-54. The church is named after the great Augustinian monastery founded here in 1253 by Humphrey de Bohun upon his return from the Crusades and was later rebuilt and enlarged in 1354. In 1381 it came under attack from Wat Tyler, the rebel leader killing those seeking sanctuary in the monastery. Later, in 1529, one of the monks, Miles Coverdale, worked on his Bible translation here. During the Reformation the monastery was shut down and the church building was used as a stable. Edward VI initiated the Dutch connection when in 1550 he gave the nave of the church to Protestant refugees fleeing religious persecution in Europe, many of whom were Dutch. At this time there was not yet a single Protestant church in the Netherlands so arguably this is the oldest Dutch language Protestant church in the world. The Dutch congregation continued its association with the church, despite being briefly exiled during the reign of Mary I.

A fire caused great damage to the building in 1862 and Edward I'Anson and William Lightly restored the church in 1863-65. A sketch of it by Van Gogh (then living in Brixton) from around 1876 can be found in the Van Gogh Museum in Amsterdam. The church was later devastated during the Blitz and the current structure was built design by Arthur Bailey in a minimal, modern style. The foundation stone was laid by Princess Irene of the Netherlands. The interior is quite unlike that of any other City church and characteristically Dutch – uncluttered, with clean modern lines. The stained glass is striking and includes the figures of William of Orange and Mary, Edward VI, St Augustine and Queen Wilhelmina. Below the communion table you can see the damaged altar stone from the original church. The organ is also Dutch and the only one of its kind in England. The Dutch still hold regular services here and as an independent and ecumenical parish the church welcomes Dutch worshippers from different religious traditions. The main service is held in Dutch every Sunday at 11am, after which coffee is served in the hall below the church.

Austin Friars, EC2; Nearest transport Bank LU;
Open Tues-Fri 11am-3pm

The Dutch Church

St Edmund King and Martyr

17. St Edmund King and Martyr

First mentioned 12th century; damaged in Great Fire, rebuilt by Wren and Hooke; interior rearranged by Butterfield 19th century

This church is dedicated to King Edmund of East Anglia (c.841-870), killed by the Danes for refusing to renounce his Christian faith. It lies on the narrow, but exceptionally busy, Lombard Street, right in the old heart of the City's banking sector. The medieval church was lost in the Great Fire and rebuilt by Wren 1670-74, although the design was probably by his able assistant Robert Hooke. The rather unusual north-south orientation was retained although building defects led to a new tower being built by Hawksmoor in 1707 and the interior was later much altered by the Victorians. This is perhaps the only surviving church in the City to have suffered damage from German bombs in both World Wars. The Germans dropped an incendiary bomb on the church in 1917, and it was only restored in the early 1930s, before further damage was caused by the Blitz in 1941.

The exterior is particularly distinctive from the approach down Lombard Street because of its tall square tower and blackened lead spire, coupled with an attractive projecting circular clock (c.1810). Inside, the dark oblong interior is rather plain and small with no aisles. The rich panelling and stained glass gives the church an atmosphere once likened to the private chapel of a nobleman's house. Despite the restorations and damage over centuries, it contains many older features including the churchwardens' pews at the rear and paintings of Moses and Aaron dating from 1833. The stained glass window behind the altar depicting Christ in Glory is thought to have been made in Germany in the 1860s and arrived in England destined for St Paul's. It is said the cathedral rejected the glass, unhappy with the angels being clothed in red rather than white, so the glass went instead to another church. After the latter was demolished in 1905 the glass ended up here as a memorial to the Duke of Clarence, eldest son of Edward VII. There are two organ cases, one from c.1701, the other a late 19th-century replica. On the west wall there is an interesting memorial to Charles Melville Hays, killed on the Titanic. Nearby is the beautifully restored font and cover. Recently the church has become home to The London Centre for Spirituality, sponsored by the Bishop of London, which aims to offer courses, meditation and discussion groups for those interested in spirituality. The Centre has injected life into what had become a rather neglected and underused place. The church now contains an excellent bookshop open from 10am-6pm Monday to Friday.

Lombard Street, EC3; Nearest transport Bank LU; Open Mon-Fri 10am-6pm

St Edmund the King and Martyr

18. St Ethelburga the Virgin

Possible Saxon origins; first recorded 1250, rebuilt 14th century; restored 17th century, survived Great Fire; destroyed by IRA bomb 1993; reopened 2002

The smallest City church is also the only Anglican church in London dedicated to St Ethelburga, 7th century Abbess of Barking Abbey. She was the daughter of Ethelbert, first Christian King of Kent, and sister to St Erkenweld, Bishop of London and founder of Barking Abbey (see All Hallows by the Tower). The original church was recorded in 1250 as 'St Adelburga' however the dedication suggests the church was probably Saxon in origin. It was rebuilt and restored several times over the centuries although having survived the Great Fire it was until recently most notable for being a rare example of what medieval City churches looked like before 1666. Until 1932 the entrance to the old church was unique in being hidden from view by two shabby shops built c.1570 to provide income for the churchwarden. Visitors had to walk through a dark tunnel between the shops in order to attend a service. Sadly the church was devastated by an IRA bomb in 1993 and the extent of the damage meant it was not reopened until 2002. Prince Charles performed the opening ceremony and the restoration was made possible through commendable fund raising efforts within the City, driven by the Bishop of London and supported by *The Times* newspaper.

Henry Hudson, 17th-century English navigator, took communion here with his crew in 1607 before setting out on an ill-fated voyage to discover the North-West Passage. Whilst the journey was unsuccessful, he did discover both the river and the bay that now bear his name. The church used to contain three commemorative windows to Hudson, given by the Hudson Bay Company, citizens of the USA and citizens of the British Empire respectively, however these were destroyed by the IRA bombing. John Larke, rector of the church from 1504-42 and close friend of St Thomas More, suffered a similar fate to his patron when he was hung drawn and quartered at Tyburn in 1544 for his defiance of Henry VIII. In the 19th century the church attracted controversy for its 'High Church' tendencies and Rector John Rodwell published the first English translation of the Qur'an in 1861.

Now a Centre for Reconciliation and Peace, the restored interior, with few original features remaining, is designed as a flexible meeting space and incorporates modern offices. A pleasant small memorial garden and fountain can be found at the rear.

Bishopsgate, EC2; Nearest transport Liverpool Street LU/Rail;
Open Wed 11am-3pm

St Ethelburga the Virgin
images from left: exterior c.1910, exterior 2005

19. St Giles Cripplegate

Possible Saxon origins; first mentioned early 11th century, rebuilt 14th century; major fire damage 1545; survived Great Fire; restored after fire damage 19th century but gutted in Blitz; re-opened 1960

St Giles appears defiantly stranded within the Barbican Centre, the vast cultural and residential estate built upon the ruins of postwar Moorfields. Before the Second World War St Giles was a mass of old timbered City buildings and streets. Dedicated to the 7th-century Greek patron saint of cripples and beggars, 'Cripplegate' actually refers to one of the gates in the city wall – the name deriving from the Saxon 'crepel' or 'cruple', meaning a covered walkway. St Giles was popular in medieval times having founded a monastery in Provence upon land given by King Wamba after the King had been moved by Giles injuring himself saving a hind from the King's hunting party. If you look up as you enter the church you will see a hind portrayed over the porch. Whilst the original church is thought to have been Saxon, the first substantial building was built c. 1090 by Alphune, Bishop of London. It was later rebuilt in a Gothic Perpendicular style c.1394, then again following a fire in 1545. St Giles escaped the Great Fire, only to be damaged by fire in 1897 and then gutted during the Blitz. Despite these misfortunes it remains one of the few late medieval churches in the City. The post-Second World War restoration was not completed until 1960, during which time St Giles stood eerily alone in the flattened area that would give rise to the Barbican. Godfrey Allen, who restored the church, was helped in his work by the discovery in Lambeth Palace of the original restoration plans drafted after the 1545 fire. The interior of this large church is essentially based upon these authentic plans.

The west end houses an imposing Jordan & Bridge organ dating from 1733, originally from St Luke's Old Street and a replacement for the Renatus Harris organ destroyed in the Blitz. Oliver Cromwell was married here in 1620, as were Sir Thomas More's parents in 1474; Sir Martin Frobisher, one of Drake's captains against the Armada and himself a famous adventurer, was buried here and has a memorial on the south wall. Daniel Defoe, author of *Robinson Crusoe*, was born in the parish and John Bunyan, author of *The Pilgrim's Progress*, used to preach here. Both men are buried in nearby Bunhill Fields, along with other dissenters of the St Giles' parish. William Holman Hunt, the Pre-Raphaelite painter, was baptized here and both poet John Milton (d.1674) and his father (also John Milton) were buried by the chancel. Rather opportunistically the Verger of 1793 charged people 6d to see the poet's body in the opened tomb – the lack of interest soon saw the price fall to 2d. A memorial stone on the floor near the pulpit marks the spot of Milton's burial place. There are busts of Bunyan, Defoe, Cromwell and Milton, and the great poet also has a bronze statue by the south wall. Elizabethan John Foxe, author of the *Book Of Martyrs*, was buried here, as was cartographer and historian John Speed (d.1629) who is remembered by a memorial on the south wall. Two of Shakespeare's nephews were christened in St Giles, and one buried here. Shakespeare's brother Edmund lived just outside the church and was later buried in Southwark Cathedral. Intriguingly on the south wall is a monument to parishioner Margaret Lucy (d.1634), great granddaughter to Sir Thomas Lucy, himself buried in the church in the same year. Sir Thomas is thought to have been the satirical inspiration for Shakespeare's Justice Swallow in *Henry IV Part II* and also *The Merry Wives of Windsor* – the legend being that the aspiring playwright fled Stratford-on-Avon to avoid a charge of poaching on Sir Thomas's country estate.

Whilst the church escaped the Great Fire of 1666, its parish did not escape the Great Plague the year before and an estimated 5-8,000 parishioners died as a result. St Giles has an active and enthusiastic congregation drawn largely from the Barbican and the immediate parish and is unique in having the first female Rector of any City church in Katharine Rumens.

Fore Street, Barbican EC2; Nearest transport Barbican and Moorgate LU/Rail, St Paul's LU; Open Mon-Fri 11am-4pm

St Giles Cripplegate

St Helen Bishopsgate

20. St Helen Bishopsgate

Possibly ancient foundations; existing church added to by nunnery early 13th century; survived Great Fire, several extensive restorations thereafter; badly damaged by IRA bombs 1992/93; reopened 1995

One of the City's few remaining medieval churches, St Helen's is tucked away off busy Bishopsgate underneath the massive Swiss Re building that now dominates the City skyline. St Helen, or Helena, was mother to the Roman Emperor Constantine, famous for converting the Roman Empire to Christianity and founding the Eastern capital of Byzantium (renamed Constantinopolis). St Helen is best remembered for her searches throughout the Holy Land during the 4th century for documentary evidence of Jesus, said to have culminated in the discovery of the 'true' cross on which he was crucified. Legend has it that St Helen once held a piece of the cross, and that Constantine, who spent several years in Britain, founded the original church on the site of a pagan temple. In about 1210 the Benedictine Priory of St Helen was founded here by William Fitzwilliam. The original parish church was rebuilt with two halves, one for parishioners and one for the nuns. You can see the evidence of this today as the exterior of the church still looks as if it is two naves joined together. The nuns were clearly less pious than the conservatism of the age might suggest – in 1385 they were chastised by the church authorities for keeping pets, kissing secular persons and wearing fancy veils. Evidently they refused to fully conform as in 1439 the nuns' 'dancing and revelling' was criticised and prohibited except at Christmas.

Henry VIII shut the Priory in 1538 during the Dissolution and it passed into the hands of a relative of Thomas Cromwell. The building was later sold to the Leathersellers' Company. The wooden screen which separated the nuns from parishioners was removed and the building became a normal parish church with the last of the original convent buildings being demolished as late as 1799. Whilst the church survived the Blitz, it was badly damaged by the IRA bombs of 1992 and 1993. In 1995 a major reordering took place that fundamentally (and controversially) changed the interior of the church so it contained for the first time a single floor at the same level. Inside, four prominent Gothic arches dating from around 1480 indicate the former dividing line between the priory and parish church. The north end contains a large number of important pre-Great Fire monuments – earning St Helen's the nickname of the 'Westminster Abbey' of the City. Many came from the 'lost' church of St Martin Outwich after it was demolished in 1874 and its parish combined with St Helen's.

Particularly worth seeing is the squint on the north wall – slots set at an angle so the nuns, unable to enter that part of the church, could stand outside and still see the altar. On the far east end is a magnificent enclosed marble monument of 1574 dedicated to Sir William Pickering, Ambassador to Spain under Elizabeth I. Nearby is the oldest surviving sword rest in the City bearing the arms of Sir John Lawrence, Lord Mayor during the Great Plague of 1665. On the near north end you can see the remains of the stained glass window that survived the IRA bombs, including one depicting Shakespeare and dating from 1884. Whilst itself unimportant, it is a reminder that Shakespeare once lived in this small parish, his name even appearing on a parish Rate Assessment of 1597. The pulpit dates from around 1630 and is beautifully carved. John Wesley twice preached from it, noting in his diary of 1738 that he 'preached at Great St Helen's, to a very numerous congregation…'. There are a number of fine 15th and 16th-century brasses on the floor, although some were defaced by the Puritans in 1644 for containing 'superstitious inscriptions'. In the north-east corner of the church is the elegant tomb of Sir Thomas Gresham (d.1579) legendary City grandee, who founded Gresham College, The Royal Exchange and gave his name to 'Gresham's law' – the economic principle that 'bad money drives out good'. Today the church has an evangelical tradition and serves as a thriving centre for Christian study groups (also looking after the nearby St Andrew Undershaft and St Peter upon Cornhill). As a result visiting times are fairly limited, but try the church office at St Helen's.

Bishopsgate, Great St Helen's, EC3; Nearest transport Liverpool Street LU/Rail; Open Mon-Fri 9.30am-12.30pm, afternoons by appointment (contact church office tel 020 7283 2231)

St Helen Bishopgate

85

86

St James Garlickhythe

21. St James Garlickhythe

First recorded 12th century, rebuilt c.1326; destroyed by Great
Fire; rebuilt by Wren; damaged in Blitz; reopened 1963

As with other churches located near the Thames, St James' has
strong connections to the sea faring trade that was crucial to
London's growth into a great commercial centre. Dedicated to
James the Apostle, or 'the Great', the remainder of the name refers
both to 'Queenhithe', a major harbour on the Thames and one of
its chief imports – garlic. In medieval times the original dedication
was to both St James and his brother St John. At that time the
Thames and its quays would have been much nearer to the church,
various embanking projects over intervening centuries having
increased the distance. Queen Isabella, wife of King John (1166-
1216), once owned the rights to dues payable on the harbour and it
is said that those who failed to pay sometimes sought sanctuary in
the church. The church was rebuilt in the 14th century and its
parish records dating from the baptism of Edward Butler in 1535 are
claimed to be the oldest in England. The church was destroyed by
the Great Fire and rebuilt by Wren between 1676-82. He created
a neat, rectangular church, upon which was later built a graceful
Baroque steeple between 1713-17 – possibly designed by
Hawksmoor. The clock on the tower contains a figure of St James,
a modern replacement of the original figure destroyed in the Blitz.

The interior contains the highest nave in the City apart from St
Paul's and many 17th-century furnishings from the 'lost' St Michael
Queenhithe. This height, coupled with Wren's large clear windows, results in the church being superbly well lit and earns St
James's the deserved nickname of 'Wren's Lantern'. The rectangular interior is pleasing; comprising a nave, aisles and chancel under
a lofty ceiling supported by Corinthian columns. The church clearly has had mixed fortunes – it narrowly missed being destroyed by
one bomb in the First World War and a 500lb bomb failed to
explode during the Second World War, although it was later damaged in the Blitz. Further misfortune befell St James when it had

to be shut from 1954-63 after the discovery of death-watch beetle in the roof timbers. There was then further damage by a freak accident in 1991 when a crane collapsed nearby and destroyed part of the south wall.

The elegant double staircase leads up to a magnificent organ of c.1718 by Johann Knoppell. It is thought originally to have been built by 'Father Smith' (Bernhard Schmidt), one of the most famous organ makers of the late 17th century. On the right of the chancel is a bust of Thomas Crammer (1489-1556), Archbishop of Canterbury under Henry VIII and burnt at the stake under Queen Mary. The church still uses Cramner's *Book of Common Prayer*. The magnificently colourful painting of the Ascension over the altar is by Andrew Geddes and dates from 1815. Nearby is a memorial credenza made out of wood from the Marchioness, the pleasure boat which sank in the Thames in 1993. The church is dotted with decorative cockle shells – symbols of the shells brought back by travellers from their pilgrimage to the Apostle's shrine at Santiago de Compostela in Spain, where the saint was taken after being martyred by the Romans in 44AD. The cathedral built to house his remains was second only to Rome in importance to the medieval pilgrim and for many centuries the Spanish army's war cry was 'Santiago!' (or 'Saint James!'). It is unclear why the shell itself became St James' symbol, however it may be because medieval pilgrims used such shells as primitive spoons or cups during their arduous travels.

Today the church is very active, hosting many fine lunchtime musical recitals and being used by ten City Livery Companies. It also has a curious legacy in that it possesses a 400 year old mummified body, once kept in a cupboard, but currently being prepared to be re-interred within the church perimeter.

Garlick Hill, EC4; Nearest transport Mansion House LU; Normally open Tues-Thurs 10.30am-3pm, however call church to check as times may vary (020 7236 1719)

St James Garlickhythe

St Katherine Cree

22. St Katherine Cree

First church c. 1280, possibly older; rebuilt 1504, largely demolished then rebuilt c.1628-31; survived Great Fire, minor damage in Blitz

St Katherine stands in the shadows of a rather soulless section of Leadenhall Street, and is particularly notable for being a rare combination of Gothic and Classical architecture dating from the reign of Charles I. The original church was built by the Priory of the Holy Trinity, itself founded by Henry I's wife, Mathilda of Scotland, who invited the Augustinian Order to take up residence in 1108. Whilst the Priory church served the parish of Christchurch, the Prior later decided to build St Katherine for the sole use of parishioners in order to prevent his canons being 'disturbed by the presence of laity'. 'Cree' is a corruption of Christ, reflecting the church's former name of St Katherine de Christchurch at Alegate – the dedication is to the saint tortured on a spiked wheel by the Romans. The Priory was the first in London to be dissolved during the reign of Henry VIII in 1531, and the church, although only recently rebuilt in 1504, was nearly totally demolished. More than a century later the church was again rebuilt, although the tower remains from the 1504 building. Before you enter, look up at the elegant sundial on the south wall which dates from 1706.

The new church was consecrated in 1631 by William Laud (1573-1645), Bishop of London, and later Archbishop of Canterbury. The Archbishop's support for Charles I resulted in Laud's conviction by Parliament on a charge of high treason, evidence of alleged 'popish' practices during St Katherine's consecration ceremony being used by the trial prosecution. Laud was executed on nearby Tower Hill – his connection with the church is still apparent in the Laud Chapel to be found in the south-east corner of the church. The chapel is to this day furnished by the Society of King Charles the Martyr, an Anglo-Catholic devotional society for those interested in the King's life and sacrifice – a small wooden figurine of Charles I stands half-way down the north aisle. The octagonal marble font on the north-east corner was presented in around 1631 by John Gayer, Lord Mayor and international merchant, and contains his arms. Gayer was threatened by a lion whilst travelling in Arabia and knelt in prayer asking the Lord for help. He survived, and to show gratitude for his deliverance donated a large sum of money to charity, requesting that a service be held here annually on the 16th October to mark the anniversary of his encounter. Today, the 'Lion Sermon' still takes place, 2005 marking the 360th anniversary of the sermon.

Particularly worth seeing is the Throckmorton Memorial just beside the Laud chapel on the south-east wall. Sir Nicholas Throckmorton (1515-71) was ambassador to France and Scotland under Elizabeth I. His daughter was a lady-in-waiting to the Queen until being disgraced for marrying the Queen's favourite, Sir Walter Raleigh. Throckmorton is buried under the floor of the church, and a corruption of his name lives on in the nearby Throgmorton Street. Hans Holbein the Younger (1497/8-1543), the German painter, is also believed to have been buried in the old church after succumbing to the plague. The beautifully carved organ case on the west end dates from 1685 and was built to house the prestigious Bernard Schmidt (or 'Father Smith') organ that both Henry Purcell and Handel are said to have played upon. If you look up, notice that the striking Gothic ribbed plaster ceiling contains the emblems and arms of the City Livery Companies that have used the church since the Great Fire.

Today, this friendly church holds regular services, and is used at the weekend by the Mar Thoma church, said to have been founded by St Thomas in AD 52 in Southern India. It also contains administrative offices for a number of charities (much to poet John Betjeman's displeasure) and hosts regular exhibitions and activities at lunchtimes.

Leadenhall Street, EC3; Nearest transport Aldgate LU; Open Mon-Fri 10.30am-4.30pm

St Katherine Cree

St Lawrence Jewry

23. St Lawrence Jewry

Original church 12th century; destroyed in Great Fire, rebuilt by Wren; damaged in Blitz, reopened 1957

Described by poet John Betjeman as 'very municipal, very splendid', St Lawrence stands imposingly on Gresham Street beside the home of the Corporation of London at Guildhall. It also stands on the former site of a 7,000 seater Roman amphitheatre, the outline of which is said to recognisable even today from the way the surrounding streets 'bend' around Guildhall. The former church graveyard forms part of the great paved open space behind the church. Unsurprisingly, the church is closely connected with the Corporation, the Lord Mayor even having his own pew for use during his frequent formal visits.

St Lawrence was martyred by the Romans in 258 AD in the presence of Emperor Valerian. Treasurer of the early church in Rome, Lawrence was ordered by the Emperor to produce its riches and responded by producing a crowd of the sick and poor. This defiance resulted in the saint being roasted to death on a gridiron, the latter becoming his symbol that can be seen if you look up to the weather vane high on the church tower. Founded in the 12th century at a time when there were 126 churches in the City, some sharing the same dedication. The name 'Jewry' distinguished this church from the rest and reflected its location at the heart of what was London's medieval Jewish area, at least until their expulsion by Edward I in 1290. The old church was destroyed by the Great Fire although some fragments of the building can be found in a cupboard by the entrance. Wren reconstructed the church in 1671-8, it is regarded as being one of his greatest creations, in addition to being his most expensive rebuild. Charles II attended the reopening and nearly 300 years later the Queen visited the church during rebuilding works after the Blitz. The Archbishop of Canterbury, Bishop of London and Lord Mayor attended the formal reopening in 1957.

The interior is suitably grand, giving the visitor a fantastic sense of space and uncluttered lavishness as befits the church of the City's 'great and good'. Brightly lit by Wren's generous windows, the interior is largely modern after the Blitz left only the walls and the tower standing. The sympathetic neo-Wren restoration was carried out to a design by Cecil Brown in 1954-7. The modern stained glass is by master glass painter Christopher Webb. It includes a commemoration to Wren and his chief craftsmen, Grinling Gibbons and Edward Strong and also to Sir Thomas More. This was once the More family's parish church, where Thomas's father was buried and where as a young lawyer Thomas lectured on St Augustine's 'City of God'. The excellent moulded and gold gilded plaster ceiling is a copy of the Wren original. The font dates from around 1620 and came from the 'lost' church of Holy Trinity Minories. In the vestibule you can see a late 16th-century painting of St Lawrence's martyrdom, attributed to de Ribera and a lucky survivor of several close encounters with the Great Fire and the Blitz. The Commonwealth chapel on the north side symbolises the City's involvement with the development of the Commonwealth, and is separated from the rest of the church by an oak screen. The St George window records those independent Commonwealth states of 1957, whilst the fine flags represent various Commonwealth countries and their armed services. The Ascension window is a gift from Auckland, New Zealand. Aside from Sir Thomas More, the church has historical connections with Sir Richard Gresham, a former Lord Mayor (1537), who was buried here. His son Sir Thomas was a close adviser to Elizabeth I, founder of The Royal Exchange and Gresham College, and lent his name to Gresham Street on whose north side the church stands. Today the church is a busy place hosting services and events for the Corporation and many Livery Companies. It also has a strong tradition of lunchtime musical recitals, played upon a massive and vibrant new German organ built by Klais of Bonn.

Gresham Street, EC2; Nearest transport Bank or St Paul's LU; Open Mon-Thurs 8am-1pm

St Lawrence Jewry

St Magnus the Martyr

24. St Magnus the Martyr

Founded late 11th century; destroyed in Great Fire, rebuilt by Wren; restored in 1920s, damaged in Blitz

This church is officially dedicated to the Norwegian Earl of Orkney (d.1116 and canonised 1135). An imposing wooden statue (1924) of the horn-helmeted saint holding a model of the building can be found on the south end of this atmospheric church on the bank of the Thames. The church actually dates from before the time of the Earl and was officially recorded in 1067. The original dedication must have been to an earlier St Magnus, perhaps the 3rd century AD Bishop of Caeserea suggested by John Stow in the 16th century. The medieval church stood on the north end of old London Bridge, one of the most important entry points into the City, and the only bridge across the Thames until Westminster Bridge was opened in 1750. The pedestrian entrance to London Bridge even went under the church tower portico after an 18th century reconstruction. Although hard to imagine now given the church's current location beside sterile office blocks and a viciously busy road, St Magnus's was once very prominent in an extremely populous part of medieval London. Thousands of people streamed across the old bridge past the church each day. A window in the south end remembers the St Thomas á Becket chapel on the bridge which paid a levy to St Magnus from the fees received by travellers crossing the bridge. This was also a place where public announcements were made and criminals punished. Until the 1970s Billingsgate Fish Market stood nearby, and its porters and noise must have contributed to the potent atmosphere. The Worshipful Company of Fishmongers continue to hold an annual service here.

Situated near to the source of the Great Fire in Pudding Lane, St Magnus was the second church to be destroyed in 1666. It was rebuilt by Wren c.1671-84, with the solid, tall steeple being added in 1705. The church clock was donated in 1709 by Lord Mayor Charles Duncombe. Legend has it that Duncombe, as a young saddler's apprentice living south of the river, was severely scolded by his employer for arriving late for work in the City. Subsequent rebuilding, including work by Charles Dance the Younger in the late 18th century, has tended to obscure the original Wren design. One example is the blocking in of the north side windows to reduce noise from the iron-rimmed carts of Billingsgate Market. The famous bridge with its houses and shops was reconstructed in the mid 18th century before being finally demolished. Its replacement was built further down the river in 1823-31 by Sir John Rennie, making St Magnus' a much quieter place.

The church has great presence, despite post Blitz restoration work. T.S Eliot, perhaps inspired by a lunchtime visit during his years as a City banker, wrote in his poem *The Waste Land* of an area 'Where fishmen lounge at noon, where the walls of Magnus Martyr hold, Inexplicable splendour of Ionian white and gold'. No doubt Eliot, who once declared that he was 'an Anglo-Catholic in religion, a classicist in literature and a royalist in politics', was drawn to the richly decorative reordering of the interior carried out in the mid-1920s by Martin Travers in Anglo-Catholic style. Later the poet was involved in protests against the proposed closure of the church. St Magnus' is also mentioned in Charles Dicken's *Oliver Twist*. When describing Nancy's rendezvous with Mr Brownlow on London Bridge, Dickens writes of 'The tower of old Saint Saviour's Church, and the spire of Saint Magnus, so long the giant-warders of the ancient bridge'.

Amongst many interesting interior features is a large model of old London Bridge just inside the entrance to the right. The organ case is notable, created in 1712 by Abraham Jordan, and the first to have a swell-box. Henry Yeule, master mason to Edward III, Richard II and Henry I, and who worked on Westminster Hall, was buried in the old church in 1400. A Victorian memorial remembers Miles Coverdale (d.1569) who assisted Tyndale in the translation of the first English Bible and who was once Rector here. His body was reburied in St Magnus' after being removed from another City church. Today the church continues to follow a 'High Church' tradition and is also the home of the Friends of the City Churches. This organisation is designed to encourage the preservation of the City churches and foster a wider awareness of their activities.

Lower Thames Street, EC3; Nearest transport Monument LU; Open Tues-Fri 9.30am-4pm, Sun 10am-1pm

St Magnus the Martyr

25. St Margaret Lothbury

First recorded late 12th century; rebuilt mid 15th century, destroyed in Great Fire; rebuilt by Wren

St Margaret's is the 'banker's church', unsurprisingly given its location behind the Bank of England. The dedication is to St Margaret of Antioch, a virgin and martyr who died under Roman persecution in the 4th century and the patron saint of women in childbirth. The meaning of 'Lothbury' is not entirely clear, however in medieval times the church name used to refer to 'upon Lothberi' or 'de Lodeburi' and this may indicate a drain or 'lode' that once connected the site to the Walbrook stream. The Abbey's Saxon foundations suggest this church's history began well before the 12th century when it was first officially recorded. The church was rebuilt in 1440 at the expense of Lord Mayor Robert Large, with whom the printer Caxton served his apprenticeship

After the Great Fire Wren rebuilt this small church (1683-92) using Portland stone. The tower was added in 1700 and is attributed by some to Wren's assistant Robert Hooke. The interior is rather dark with rich wood furnishings from 'lost' City churches. The splendid original Wren wooden chancel screen (c. 1684) was brought from All Hallows the Great after the latter was demolished in 1894. The screen is one of only two surviving original Wren screens (the other being in St Peter upon Cornhill). The font cover and reredos on the south aisle came from St Olave Jewry, whilst the painting in the sanctuary of Moses and Aaron (c.1700) came from St Christopher Le Stocks. The fine organ was built by George England and was also originally from St Olave's. Although restored in 1984, it retains its original case and much of its original pipe work. The superbly carved font is attributed to Grinling Gibbons.

Today, the church hosts energetic evangelical lunchtime services and gatherings and many musical recitals. It is also a popular place for services for those in the banking profession and is the church of five City Livery Companies.

Lothbury, EC2; Nearest transport Bank LU; Open Mon-Fri 7am-6pm

HONI · SOIT · QUI · MAL · Y · PENSE

Sir Wm

Clayton
Kt.

St Margaret Lothbury

St Margaret Pattens

26. St Margaret Pattens

First recorded 12th century; rebuilt 1538; destroyed in Great Fire and rebuilt by Wren; reordered 1880; some damage during Blitz; reopened 1956

This tall, elegant Wren church was praised by former Archbishop of Canterbury Dr Robert Runcie for its 'mixture of simplicity and splendour, formality and friendliness'. Despite the anonymous office blocks that have crept up around it in the last few years, St Margaret's spire is still an imposing sight as you walk down Eastcheap. Completed in 1702 to a height of 199 feet, the spire is the third highest of the City churches. The dedication is to St Margaret of Antioch (see St Margaret Lothbury) and 'pattens' refers to tall wooden clogs, which strapped to the feet of medieval Londoners allowing them to wade through the debris of the City. The artisans who made the pattens worked nearby in Rood Lane, hence their association with the church. Since the 15th century the City's Worshipful Company of Pattenmakers has had strong ties with the church, although the last working pattenmaker is thought to have died in the 19th century. The names of past masters of the Company can be found on the south wall, along with a depiction of the pattens themselves on the window above. There is a similar commemorative window to the Worshipful Company of Basketmakers which also has a long-standing connection to the church.

Rood Lane beside the church was once called St Margaret Pattens Lane, but when the church was rebuilt in the 16th century a cross (or 'rood') was put up outside – those who prayed to it (and contributed to the cost of rebuilding) received a pardon from the Pope for their sins. During the Reformation such practices were frowned upon and the rood was destroyed, but not before lending its name to the lane.

As you enter the church stop to look at the two canopied pews, unique in the City, on either side of the nave entrance. These were for the churchwardens and the initials on either side reflect the name not only of this church, but also St Gabriel Fenchurch

('SGF'). St Gabriel's was not rebuilt after the Great Fire and was instead amalgamated with St Margaret's. Given the strong rivalry between parishes at this time it is likely that the division between the churchwardens in their own respective pews was more than simply physical for many years after 1666. Although hard to see, the inside roof of the southern canopied pew contains the initials 'CW 1686', said to be those of Sir Christopher Wren who rebuilt the church in 1684-87. Whilst Wren was known to have worshipped here regularly, the retired architect who showed me around doubted if the story was true as in his view any architect worth their salt would never have put their name in such an obscure place.

The Stuart royal arms above the door are a particularly fine example. The massive copper cross on the middle of the south wall, said to be a copy of the cross on St Paul's Cathedral, once topped the spire, but proved to be too heavy and was taken down. The 1749 organ that dominates the west end is still in use, whilst the reredos behind the altar contains a 17th-century painting of Christ in Gethsemane attributed to Carlo Maratta (1625-1713). If you look closely at the finely carved wooden pulpit, you can see an hourglass holder. The church still has an hour glass dating from 1750 which was used to time sermons. Sadly the 'punishment table' for unruly children mentioned in a number of guide books was stolen several years ago, however the south end has the original hooks upon which male parishioners would hang their wigs.

On the south wall just under the cross is a memorial to Charles I – an annual service used to be held here in his memory. On the floor nearby is an interesting memorial to James Donaldson, the 'City Garbler' (d 1685), who was entrusted with checking the quality of spices sold in the Square Mile. The 19th-century reredos in the north aisle chapel incorporates a Della Robbia style tondo commemorating former rector Thomas Wagstaffe. He was deprived of his position for supporting James II over William III – a further reminder of this church's affiliation to the Stuart dynasty as noted above with the families arms still intact at the entrance.

Today the church is a busy place at lunchtimes, hosting a variety of congregations. This includes a slimming club for workers seeking an alternative to the expensive City gyms. If you ask one of the very helpful attendants they may also show you a pair of pattens kept in the church (see below).

Rood Lane off Eastcheap, Eastcheap, EC3; Nearest transport Monument or Tower Hill LU; Open Mon-Fri 10.30am-4pm

St Martin within Ludgate

27. St Martin within Ludgate

First recorded c.1138 although possibly much older; destroyed in Great Fire and rebuilt by Wren

From Ludgate Circus the famous view to the east of St Paul's is intersected by the beautiful lead Wren steeple of St Martin's up on Ludgate Hill. St Martin's is dedicated to the soldier and Bishop of Tours who died in the 4th century. Legend has it that the original church was founded by the Welsh hero-king Cadwallon in the 7th century. Until the Dissolution of the Monasteries the church belonged to the Abbey and Convent of Westminster. The church, was built inside (or 'within') the old City Wall and stood opposite the western entry point into the City at Ludgate until the latter was demolished in 1760.

The slim Portland stone exterior facing onto Ludgate Hill was designed by Wren to be best seen from the side. The tower's octagonal, lead-covered cupola supports a balcony, and above that a lantern under the lead-covered spire with a ball and vane. The modest scale of the façade does not prepare you for the magnificent interior, tall and cruciform in shape. To get there you must first walk through a large entrance lobby, and then under a screen with carved door cases. This was designed to offer the congregation some protection from the traffic noise immediately outside on Ludgate Hill. Once inside you discover one of Wren's least altered church interiors (1677-86), with fine dark woodwork that largely escaped the Blitz. There is some evidence the principal design was by Wren's assistant Robert Hooke, recorded as having visited the church 31 times. Hooke's interest in Dutch architecture may explain what is sometimes described as the 'continental' feel of the exterior.

Principal points of interest include the fine reredos behind the altar illustrating the Lord's Prayer, Ten Commandments and Creed. High above the Greek cross in the centre of the floor is a grand 17th-century chandelier which was brought from St Vincent's Cathedral in the Caribbean. The font dates from 1673 and contains the Greek palindrome 'Niyon anomhma mh monan oyin', or 'cleanse my sin and not my face only', copied from the Cathedral of St Sophia in Constantinople. On the north end is a bell dating from 1693 standing on an iron chest and beside it original shelves which were used to distribute bread to the poor. The pictures on either side of the altar are of Saints Mary Magdalene, Martin and Gregory. William Sevenoake, found abandoned as a child in the Kent town that gave him his adopted name, was buried in the old church. He went on to become a wealthy merchant and friend of Henry V, serving as Lord Mayor in 1418 and founding the prestigious Sevenoaks School in his home town.

The church retains the original box pews, although they were shortened and made into benches in 1894-95, an interesting result being that the four columns appear much taller than originally intended. Rector and travel writer Samuel Purchas of the old church was said to have been a friend to American Indian Princess Pocahontas (1595-1617). Pocahontas famously saved the life of Captain John Smith, leader of the settlement of Jamestown in Virginia. She later married another settler, John Rolfe, who took his wife back to England where she became a celebrity and was received by the King and Queen. Pocahontas was known to have stayed in accommodation beside St Martin's c. 1616 and is likely to have visited her friend the rector there.

Today, the church is a Guild Church hosting a weekly service and frequent musical recitals. It is also particularly popular during the Christmas period when the City institutions book it up months in advance for their carol concerts.

Ludgate Hill, EC4; Nearest transport St Paul's LU; Open Mon-Fri 10am-4pm

28. St Mary Abchurch

First mentioned 12th century, destroyed in Great Fire; rebuilt by Wren; damaged in Blitz, restored by Godfrey Allen 1945-57

This is one of Wren's greatest parish churches, perhaps only St Stephen Walbrook being of equal or greater stature. It is certainly one of the most memorable City churches, principally because on the first visit it is difficult to find, but once reached is a delight inside. Dedicated to the Virgin Mary, the meaning of 'Abchurch' is unclear. It has been suggested the name refers to a forgotten benefactor named Abba, or is a corruption of the older name 'Upchurch', itself perhaps derived from the fact that members of the 12th-century St Mary Overies Priory (on the site of Southwark Cathedral) would have had to look 'up' the hill to see the church they controlled. After the Reformation Elizabeth I was persuaded to give the patronage or 'living' of the church to the Master of Corpus Christi College Cambridge, who retains the right to appoint the rector to this day.

St Mary's is found halfway down the narrow Abchurch Lane that links Cannon Street and King William Street. The visitor suddenly finds themself coming out into the open area of Abchurch Yard, a former burial ground whose boundaries are still marked by posts. To stand in the Yard and look at the Dutch influenced red brick exterior, it is not hard to imagine yourself in the City of the 17th century – an oasis of calm away from busy Cannon Street nearby. The interior is almost square, its rich dark woodwork contributing to the intimate atmosphere. Built 1681-86, it is often said to be one of the least altered of Wren's churches and employed the skills of some of his finest craftsmen. It is certainly one of the most original churches, particularly the beautiful dome not hinted at from the outside, which comes as a surprise for the first time visitor. The dome was built during Wren's experimental period, later perfected in the much larger version of St Paul's. Of the existing City churches only St Stephen Walbrook has a dome of similar quality. The dramatic painting on the dome was added in 1708 by parishioner William Snow and contains a heavenly choir around the name of God in Hebrew. The pulpit (c.1685) is by William Grey and is one of the finest examples in any City church. William Emmett made the wooden Royal Arms, lion and unicorn and font cover. Near the entrance of the church is an original alms box dating from 1694 and the wrought iron sword holders by the front pews carry the arms of two Lord Mayors who were parishioners c. 1812 & 1814.

The beautiful reredos features limewood carvings by Grinling Gibbons, the pre-eminent carver of his generation. The receipt dating from 1686 for Gibbons' huge 'olter pees' is kept in the Guildhall Library, making St Mary's the only city church other than St Paul's that can actually document work attributed to Wren's master carver. The reredos was broken into nearly two thousand pieces during the Blitz, and it took five years to piece the jigsaw together. The pelican in the centre represents the Eucharist and is also the crest of Corpus Christi College. Also of note are the original box pews on three sides of the church. In Wren's time children and servants would have sat at these ends, able to keep their dogs underneath the pews in special cupboards. The latter were sadly removed after the Second World War.

The west gallery was once reserved for pupils at Merchant Taylors' School which stood on nearby Suffolk Lane until 1875. Because of Blitz damage the original organ was replaced, but the carved oak case dates from 1717 and was originally housed in All Hallows Bread Street until it was demolished in 1877. During the Blitz the church was damaged and a flagstone in the churchyard was broken. Underneath was discovered evidence of previously unknown vaults dating from the 14th and 17th centuries. Today, the church is a Guild Church and is normally very quiet. It continues to have an association with the Fruiterers' Company, whose arms you can see on the South window.

Abchurch Lane, EC4; Nearest transport Bank or Monument LU, Cannon St LU/Rail; Open Tues 10am-3pm, Wed 12noon-2pm

St Mary Abchurch

St Mary Aldermary

29. St Mary Aldermary

Saxon origins likely, first recorded 11th century; rebuilt 16th and 17th centuries; damaged in Great Fire and rebuilt by Wren; partially rebuilt 1788; restored various times in 19th century

St Mary's is an oddity – a 'Gothic' Wren church. Dedicated to the Virgin, 'Aldermary' means 'older Mary' in old English. It was probably intended to distinguish the church from nearby St Mary le Bow and other, now demolished, churches with the same dedication. The church lies at the end of a maze of old City lanes to the north, whilst the south side was largely hidden from view until being exposed during the building of Queen Victoria Street in the 1860s. First mentioned in around 1080, the church probably has Saxon origins and was later rebuilt c.1510 under the patronage of grocer and Lord Mayor Henry Keble. Only the tower and some walls survived the Great Fire although it is unclear why Wren chose to rebuild the church (1679-82) in an uncharacteristically Gothic style. The funding for the reconstruction came from the will of Henry Rodgers, and his niece Anne. Despite some rather difficult litigation brought by her fellow executors, £5,000 was eventually paid by the niece to fund the works. This may have been on the condition that the style of the damaged church be retained, or Wren may have been under pressure from parishioners. Whatever the cause, the fortunate result is arguably the most important late 17th-century Gothic church in England.

As you enter, the most striking feature is the fabulously lofty fan-vaulted ceiling. This is a feature normally reserved for cathedrals and St Mary's is the only parish church in England known to have one. The tower that survived the Great Fire did not survive the lesser known Great Storm of 1703 and was replaced with the existing structure. The Victorians greatly altered Wren's interior during restorations in the 1870s in what poet John Betjeman described as a 'heavy-handed effort' to make the interior appear authentically medieval. Despite the loss of many original furnishings the pulpit is original and believed to have been carved by Grinling Gibbons, whilst the rare wooden sword rest dates from 1682. The west door case was taken from the 'lost' church of St Antholin's, whilst the organ was built by George England in 1781. Richard Chaucer, 14th-century vintner and relative of medieval poet Geoffrey Chaucer, was buried in the old church and poet John Milton married his third wife here in 1663. There is also a monument on the south wall to Sir Percivall Pott, eminent 18th-century surgeon of St Bartholomew's Hospital, whose patients included Samuel Johnson and Thomas Gainsborough. Pott was inspired to write the influential *Treatise on Ruptures* after being thrown from his horse in 1756 and invented the medical term 'Pott's fracture'. There are interesting monuments to John Seale on the north wall, and also to Rene Baudouin and James Braidwood. After damage during the Blitz, the church was restored by Arthur Nisbet and St Mary's became a Guild Church in 1954.

Bow Lane, EC4; Nearest transport Mansion House LU; Open Mon, Tues, Thurs and 1st and 3rd Wed 11am-3pm

St Mary Aldermary

30. St Mary le Bow

Ancient origins; first recorded late 11th century; destroyed in
Great Fire; rebuilt by Wren; destroyed in Blitz, reopened 1964

This is one of the best known City churches, partly because of the
London tradition that a true Cockney must be born 'within the
sound of Bow bells' (or alternatively within the sound of the bells
of this church and Bow church in the East End). The foundations
of St Mary's lie on the remains of a Roman basilica and the fact the
church was first recorded in late 11th century suggests its origins are
Saxon. The church's medieval Latin name of 'Sancta Maria de
Arcubus' refers to the arches still to be found in the crypt. This is
where the Archbishop of Canterbury's ecclesiastical Court of Arches
has been held from medieval times to this day. All bishops in the
Province of Canterbury take their oath of allegiance here in the
presence of the Archbishop. The arched crypt is the earliest example found in any London church and was created by Lanfranc of
Canterbury when he rebuilt the church in the 11th century. It is
the sole surviving feature of the pre-Wren church, and part of it is
now occupied by one of the best vegetarian restaurants in the City.

This church has never been a stranger to drama. In 1091 the
roof blew off and in 1271 the steeple collapsed, in each case killing
several parishioners. In 1284 an alleged criminal attempted to
claim the ancient right of sanctuary inside the church but was
lynched by a mob. This resulted in 16 men being hung, drawn and
quartered and one woman burnt at the stake. The church itself had
to be closed, its doors and windows ritually sealed with thorns,
until it could be reconsecrated. In 1331 a balcony collapsed during a jousting tournament to celebrate the birth of the Black
Prince causing Queen Philippa and her attendants to fall to the
ground. Wren placed an iron balcony on the tower, still visible
today, as a memento. After being destroyed in the Great Fire, this
was one of the first churches to be rebuilt by Wren in 1670-80, as
well as one of the most expensive. Wren introduced an innovative
Neoclassical plan, said to have been based on the Basilica of

Maxentius in Rome. He placed the tower so that it would be a prominent landmark on busy Cheapside. The magnificent 224 feet baroque tower and Portland stone steeple was the first of its kind in London. Crowned by a distinctive dragon weather vane dating from 1679, the steeple is the tallest of all the City churches with the exception of St Bride's.

After being gutted during the Blitz, rebuilding was carried out in 1956-64 by Laurence King following Wren's original designs, but introducing a very contemporary feel. Only the outer walls and bell tower from Wren's building remain. The interior is almost square, with a central nave and aisles, and a chancel area opened up into the main body of the church. This is emphatically a modern, progressive church, with bright stained glass by John Hayward. The twin pulpits – reflecting early church tradition that the Old and New testaments were read from one side, and the Gospel from the other – are now used to host conversations and dialogues, often attracting famous speakers. There is a monument and bust on the west wall to Admiral Arthur Phillip (d.1814), first governor of Australia. The bust was brought here after being discovered during the Blitz in the burnt out shell of St Mildred's church in Bread Street, the nearby street where Phillip was born. A special commemorative service is held here each year on Australia Day. There is also a memorial in the chapel on the north end commemorating members of the Norwegian resistance during the Second World War. The memorial refers to the radio broadcasts of St Mary's bells that served as a symbol of hope for people in occupied Europe secretly listening to the BBC. The suspended rood cross comes from Oberammergau in Germany, given after the war as a symbol of reconciliation.

The significance to Londoners of Bow bells dates back to medieval times when they were rung to mark curfew and the end of the apprentices' day. They were also the bells that famously called 'Turn again, Whittington, Lord Mayor of London' to a young Dick Whittington as he rested on a Highgate milestone. According to pantomime legend Whittington did return and went on to become the City's most famous mayor. The bells are also referred to in the famous nursery rhyme *Oranges and Lemons*.

The restoration and recasting of the bells in 1933 is said to have been funded by the American entrepreneur H Gordon Selfridge. Unfortunately the restoration was short-lived, the bells being shattered during the Blitz. After the Second World War the metal salvaged from the destroyed bells was used in a new casting and the current bells were rung for the first time in 1961.

The exterior is best viewed from the pleasant courtyard that contains an excellent mid-week flower stall and a fine memorial to Captain John Smith (1580-1631). Smith, born nearby, originally worked as one of the cordwainers who plied their trade in this part of the City. He went on to become Governor of Virginia and Admiral of New England and was famously saved from death by Princess Pocahontas. The church has another strong American connection in its links to Trinity church in the heart of New York's own financial district on Wall Street. Trinity was founded in 1697, the Bishop of London's charter stating that '*All shall be ordered as it is in the Church of St Mary le Bow*'. Trinity contributed financially to the post-war rebuilding of St Mary le Bow, and after the 9/11 attack on the World Trade Centre (which stood in Trinity's parish), St Mary's organised a book of condolence for its sister church. Today, St Mary's is a very active place, hosting many recitals and exhibitions. *Cheapside, EC2; Nearest transport Bank or St Paul's LU; Open 7.30am-6pm weekdays except Fri when closes 4pm*

St Mary le Bow

31. St Mary at Hill

First mentioned 12th century, damaged in Great Fire and rebuilt by Wren, tower rebuilt 1780; further alterations 19th century, damaged by fire 1988

This small, beautiful church, is to be found crowded in by other buildings half way along the tiny winding Lovat Lane. The area gives the visitor a good impression of how the old City would have appeared before much of it was altered during the 19th century. St Mary's was first mentioned c. 1177, and Elizabethan historian John Stow suggested Thomas á Becket was once curate here. St Mary's was later rebuilt in the 15th century, before being badly damaged in the Great Fire that started in nearby Pudding Lane. Wren restored the church in 1670-74 incorporating most of the damaged structure including the tower. The tower and west side were rebuilt in the 1780s, and further rebuilding and restoration was carried out on a number of occasions in the 19th century. Largely surviving the Blitz, the church was regarded as having one of the best remaining Wren interiors of all the City churches. Regrettably, a terrible fire in 1988 caused enormous damage, including to the rare box pews. Today the restoration work is nearly complete and has been successful, although the interior still feels very bare without pews, altar or reredos. The church is almost square in outline and contains an attractive vaulted ceiling and shallow dome that rests on four free-standing columns in a Byzantine plan. The newly restored organ is particularly notable as it was designed, although never played, by Mendelssohn. The south wall contains a curious wall monument to William Old (d.1824) and his 'relict' Mary Old.

Visitors who come in through the Lovat Lane entrance should also walk around the corner to see the back of the church with its superb clock that hangs over the street named (confusingly) St Mary at Hill. That the church is still here at all is remarkable. In 1894 it was nearly demolished to help build the London Underground, and 3,000 bodies were taken from the crypt to Norwood Cemetery, in preparation for its destruction.

St Mary's was once known as the 'Fish Church' as a result of its strong connection with nearby Billingsgate Fish Market. Today the Fish Harvest Festival is still held here in October, despite the market's move to the Docklands. Afterwards the traditional 39 varieties of fish laid out during the festival are distributed to Church Army homes.

Lovat Lane, Eastcheap, EC3; Nearest transport Monument or Tower Hill LU; Open Mon-Fri 11am-4pm

St Mary at Hill

32. St Mary Moorfields
Built 1899-1903 by George Sherrin

This rather anonymous building is the only Roman Catholic church within the City boundaries. The unostentatious design is understandable given the hostility faced by the City's Roman Catholics over the centuries. This church, together with its predecessors, played an important part in the gradual public re-emergence of the Roman Catholic faith in London after the Reformation. 'Moorfields' refers to the medieval open space or moor, then on the outskirts of the City, that was gradually built upon by Londoners. A Roman Catholic chapel survived in this area for a few years in the 1680s before being suspended. In the 1730s the congregation began to meet quietly in a house in Ropemakers' Alley before this chapel was destroyed during the anti-Catholic Gordon Riots of 1780. An account of which was later given in Dickens' *Barnaby Rudge* (1841). A subsequent chapel in White Street was replaced by a grand new Classical church in Finsbury Square that was opened in 1820 and designed by John Newman. This church was the original St Mary's and later served as the temporary Roman Catholic Cathedral before Westminster Cathedral was opened.

In the late 19th century there was a diminishing number of people living in the City and St Mary's had became too large for its congregation. It was demolished in 1899 and the site sold to help pay for the building of Westminster Cathedral. The façade of the demolished church can be imagined today by visiting St John the Baptist Church in Brighton which was partially modelled on old St Mary's. The current church, retaining the name of its more illustrious predecessor, was built on a smaller site nearby in Eldon Street and opened in 1903. It was designed by George Sherrin who also worked on the dome of Brompton Oratory. It is easy to walk past the Portland Stone frontage of St Mary's without noticing it amongst the neighbouring shop fronts, however the interior is surprisingly large, although not particularly memorable and dimly lit through the meagre windows high above. The Corinthian columns around the altar are from the old church and the grand marble sarcophagus altar (c.1820) was originally intended to act as the resting place for Cardinal Wiseman. A mosaic depicting the beheading of Sir Thomas More can be seen over the entrance to the north-west chapel dedicated to this famous opponent of the English Reformation.

Today St Mary's is a busy church, with a large and active congregation. It only became a 'City church' when the City boundary was moved in 1994.

Finsbury Circus, Eldon Street EC2; Nearest transport Moorgate and Liverpool Street LU/Rail; Open Mon-Fri 7am-6.30pm

St Mary Woolnoth

33. St Mary Woolnoth

First mentioned 1191 although Saxon origins likely; rebuilt mid 15th century; damaged in Great Fire, restored by Wren but later rebuilt by Hawksmoor 18th century

Dedicated to the Virgin Mary and originally known as St Mary of the Nativity, this church is notable for being the only remaining complete City church by Wren's gifted assistant, Nicholas Hawksmoor. It is also the only City church to have survived the Second World War unscathed. Situated in a prominent part of the City at the junction of Lombard Street and King William Street, this site once contained a Roman temple to Concord. Tradition has it that the earliest recorded 12th-century church was founded here by Wulfnoth, a Saxon noble, whose name has been corrupted to form 'Woolnoth'. Alternatively, the name may refer to a local medieval wool market. In any event, the original church was replaced in 1438, and later damaged during the Great Fire. Wren may have restored it in 1670-75, although the work could have been under the direction of Sir Robert Vyner. The result was not structurally safe and Hawksmoor built the current church between 1716-27 as one of Queen Anne's 'fifty new churches', employing a magnificent English Baroque design that was equal to anything being built at the time in Europe. The exterior, with its flat topped turrets, is often regarded as being the most original in the City. The north end facing onto Lombard Street is particularly notable. The side facing King William Street is plainer, reflecting the fact it was hemmed in by other buildings when originally built by Hawksmoor.

The tranquil interior is small and square, regarded by Simon Jenkins as the 'most remarkable in the City in the majesty it conjures from a limited space'. It contains 12 giant Corinthian columns in clusters of three at the edges of the nave. The design is said to have been based by Hawksmoor on the Egyptian Hall described by Vitruvius, the 1st-century Roman architect whose *De Architectura* was printed as a book in the 15th century and became enormously influential among architects. Whilst the reredos, pulpit and plaster ceiling are original Hawksmoor furnishings, William Butterfield altered much of rest in the 1870s, including the removal of the galleries and cutting down the box pews.

John Newton was rector here from 1779-1807, and co-wrote with Cowper the hymn 'Amazing Grace'. Newton's preaching against the slave trade he was once part of greatly inspired abolitionist William Wilberforce. Newton used the pulpit that is still stands in the church. The memorial to him on the north wall records a difficult time in his younger life when he was 'once an infidel and libertine, a servant of slaves in Africa'. There is also a memorial from 1931 to Edward Lloyd, founder of the Lloyd's coffee house that gave birth to today's Lloyd's underwriting centre, who was buried here in 1712. Simon Eyre, founder of Leadenhall Market nearby, was also buried here in 1445.

The church is, like St Magnus the Martyr, referred to in T.S. Elliot's *The Wasteland*. Elliot describes crowds moving over London Bridge before they 'Flowed up the hill and down King William Street, To where St Mary Woolnoth kept the hours, With a dead sound on the final stroke of nine.' St Mary's, as with several other City churches, narrowly escaped being demolished to make way for London Underground in the 1890s. The church was saved with a compromise – Bank station's booking office was opened in the church's crypt and the doorway on the north west side was once a station entrance. Today St Mary's is a Guild Church.

Lombard Street, EC3; Nearest transport Bank LU; Open Mon-Fri 9.30am-4.30pm

34. St Michael Cornhill

Saxon origins, first mentioned 11th century; destroyed in Great Fire; tower rebuilt by Hawksmoor c.1721; restored c.1860

Dedicated to the Archangel, the first building on this site was Saxon although the earliest record dates from 1055 when the Evesham Chronicle mentions the 'living' was given to the Abbot and Convent of Evesham. The tower was later reconstructed in 1421, but the Great Fire destroyed the medieval church and it was rebuilt in a classical style (1669-72). It may have been the work of Wren, although Pevsner believes the parish may have organised the work without Wren's office being involved. The 15th-century tower was rebuilt in 1715-22 in a Gothic style, later added to by Hawksmoor in 1718-22 to a design possibly based upon that of Magdalen College, Oxford.

The church is known today as being the best 'Victorian' church in the City, attributable to the then controversial rebuilding carried out by Sir Gilbert George Scott in 1857-60. In one of the first major Victorian reorderings of the City churches, Scott replaced nearly all the 17th-century furnishings and also rebuilt the now dramatic street entrance that shows St Michael above the door disputing the body of Moses with Satan. The bronze statue of St Michael by RR Goulden commemorates the dead of the Great War. Inside, Scott's Italianate reredos behind the altar incorporates two 17th-century paintings of Aaron and Moses. The beautiful carving of the Pelican in her Piety feeding its young under the west window dates from 1775 and was originally part of the earlier reredos. The pew ends are carved with plants and herbs mentioned in the Bible and are by noted Victorian woodcarver W Gibbs Rogers. Thomas Gray, the poet who once declined the chance to become Poet Laureate, was christened here in 1716.

St Michael's has a reputation for music, its first organ dated from c.1460 and several prominent musicians have acted as the church's Director of Music over the centuries, including Richard Limpus, founder of the Royal College of Organists. Henry Purcell gave a recital on the church organ in 1684, and the tradition of lunchtime recitals, now widespread throughout the City churches, was begun here in 1916 by composer Harold Darke. The church even has a charity, the St Michael Cornhill Music Trust, established to promote the musical tradition of the church and contribute to the musical life of the City.

Just outside the church is the site of London's first coffee house (now the site of the Jamaica Wine House), run out of a tent in the church grounds in 1657 by Pasqua Rosee, servant of a Turkish merchant. The meeting of men of commerce in the early coffee houses became a crucial part of London's development as a great commercial centre, and the beginning of the great City financial institutions.

When walking past the City's numerous coffee shops full of businessmen today, you could be forgiven for thinking nothing has really changed. The church also continues its tradition of fine church music with regular lunchtime recitals, making this a busy and lively place of worship.

Cornhill, EC3; Nearest transport Bank LU;
Open Mon-Fri 8.30am-5pm

St Michael Cornhill

St Michael Paternoster Royal

35. St Michael Paternoster Royal

First mentioned early 12th century; rebuilt early 15th century by 'Dick' Whittington; destroyed by Great Fire and rebuilt by Wren; damaged 1944, reopened 1968

Dedicated to the Archangel, the use of 'paternoster' in the name of this church is possibly derived from the medieval rosary makers who worked nearby in Paternoster Row. The rosary, brought back to Europe by Crusaders, consists of a number of beads including the large Paternoster (or 'Lord's Prayer') bead. 'Royal' is thought to be a corruption of 'La Riole', the former name of College Street which runs alongside the church, and which was once inhabited by merchants who imported wine into a nearby wharf from La Reole near Bordeaux. The area around the church is also known as 'Vintry', again signalling the area's former connection with the French wine trade.

The church is best known for being associated with Sir Richard Whittington (c.1358-1423), merchant, philanthropist and Lord Mayor of London on four occasions. He lived on College Hill and paid for the church to be rebuilt in 1409. The 'Dick Whittington' of the English pantomime is far removed from story of the real Sir Richard, who was the son of a knight and became an important financier to Henry IV and V. The legend of Dick and his cat first grew from a play and ballad from 1605, however the only similarity between it and the historical facts seems to be that Richard and Dick both married Alice Fitzwaryn. He was buried on the south side of the altar beside his wife.

Following damage by the Great Fire, master mason Edward Strong rebuilt the church under Wren's supervision (1685-94). This was one of Wren's last City churches, the result being a small, simple yet elegant structure. The majestic steeple, with its three stage octagonal lantern, was added later c.1713, possibly by Wren's pupil Hawksmoor. The interior was later rearranged by William Butterfield in 1866. Destruction by a German flying bomb left just the walls and tower and exposed the previously hidden church to public view. The building was one of the last City churches to be reopened after the Second World War, with the west end truncated slightly to incorporate modern office space. Prince Philip attended the reopening ceremony, appropriate given the church's sea-faring connections.

The interior of this quiet church contains several items of interest despite the Blitz damage. The massive candelabra hanging from the ceiling dates from 1644 and once belonged to All Hallows the Great which was demolished in 1893. The strikingly coloured modern windows from 1968 are by John Hayward, with images including Whittington and his legendary cat, the streets of London paved with gold and also St Michael. Much of the 17th-century woodwork has also survived, including the font cover, altarpiece, sword rests and statues of Moses and Aaron by the altar. The pulpit is also attributed to Grinling Gibbons. In 1601 Peter Blundell, founder of Blundell's School, was buried here.

St Michael's is currently a Guild Church and serves as the headquarters for The Mission to Seafarers. The Mission assists over 300 chaplains working in ports around the world and has The Princess Royal as its president.

College Hill, EC4; Nearest transport Cannon Street LU/Rail and Monument LU; Open Mon-Fri 9am-5pm

St Michael Paternoster Royal

36. St Nicholas Cole Abbey

First recorded early 12th century; destroyed in Great Fire; rebuilt by Wren; damaged in Blitz and reopened 1962.

Lying in the shadow of St Paul's, this church is dedicated to the famous 'Santa Claus', the patron saint of children, travellers at sea, and those confronted by danger. Despite various theories, the origin of the name 'Cole Abbey' is obscure. The medieval church had close connections with the fish trade after a fish market was established nearby during the reign of Richard I and Old Fish Street once led up to the church before the building of Queen Victoria Street. A large number of fishmongers are known to have been buried here during the 16th century. One Elizabethan fishmonger left a bequest of £900 in order to construct a cistern in the north wall to allow fish to be cleaned. When Queen Victoria Street was built over the old churchyard in 1871 the old north entrance was closed, replaced by the current entrance on the south side.

The church once had strong Roman Catholic connections, being the first in London in 1553 to celebrate Mass after Queen Mary I came to the throne and attempted to restore the old faith. The church later became a Puritan stronghold in the 17th century under the patronage of Colonel Hacker, commander of the guard at the execution of Charles I. In the late 19th century, rector and Christian Socialist Henry Shuttleworth made the church a centre for topical debate, although the drinks bar he introduced is no longer operational. George Bernard Shaw is thought to have used the rector as the model for the socialist priest Mr Morell in the play *Candida*.

This was the first church to be rebuilt by Wren after the Great Fire (1672–78) and he used a simple classical design which ran against the then prevailing Gothic trend. The brick and stone exterior has tall windows and a square tower, the steeple topped by an interesting ship-design weather vane that originally came from the 'lost' church of St Michael Queenhithe. The rebuilding by Wren cost over £5,000 and the bill included 'Dinner for Dr Wren' and 'Half a pint of canary for Dr Wren's coachmen'.

St Nicholas Cole Abbey

The Blitz destroyed many valuable treasures, including carvings by Grinling Gibbons and the stained glass windows. As a result the interior is rather plain, although a candelabra, sword rest, and 16th-century lectern and painting of Jesus as a child were recovered. If you watch the 1951 Ealing comedy film *The Lavender Hill Mob* carefully, a robbery is staged outside the church and the extent of the Blitz devastation is evident. The restoration was completed in a design sympathetic to Wren's original by Arthur Bailey in 1962 and the modern stained glass windows are by Keith New. The Free Church of Scotland used the church until 2003. Unfortunately, since then it has been closed to the public.

Queen Victoria Street, EC4; Nearest transport Blackfriars and CannonStreet LU/Rail, Mansion House LU

St. OLAVE'S CHUR

St Olave Hart Street

37. St Olave Hart Street

First recorded late 12th century but likely earlier origins; rebuilt 15th century; escaped Great Fire, damaged in Blitz; reopened 1954

This small, fascinating church is dedicated to Olave (or Olaf) Haraldson, the martyred king and patron saint of Norway. He came to England to help Ethelred (the Unready) against the Danes, and in one particularly heroic action in 1014 engaged the enemy in the Battle of London Bridge. Whilst Olave's actions resulted in part of the Bridge being destroyed, he saved London, restored Ethelred to his throne, and inspired the famous nursery rhyme *London Bridge is Falling Down*. Whilst there were once three City churches with a similar dedication to this popular saviour of London, this is the sole survivor, described by poet John Betjeman as being like a 'country church'. The original church was probably made from wood and predated the first officially recorded building of the late 12th century. Today only the crypt remains from that medieval period. The current building dates from c. 1450 when it was commissioned in a Perpendicular style by wealthy parishioners including Robert and Richard Cely. It then stood beside the great monastery of the Crutched Friars, one of the most important religious orders in pre-Reformation London. The friars received their name through their custom of carrying in one hand a wooden staff surmounted by a cross. The Order can still be found today in the Netherlands.

St Olave's is one of only eight remaining churches that escaped the Great Fire of 1666. It was during this period that diarist Samuel Pepys attended the church with his wife Elizabeth after Pepys became 'Clerk of Acts' and lived in the Navy Office on the site of Seething Gardens opposite. Pepys referred to St Olave's as 'our own church' and used the exclusive Navy Office pew in the south gallery. The gallery was reached from a now lost exterior staircase from the churchyard. It was built by Pepys so he could arrive from the Navy Office without getting wet in the rain. The entrance to this staircase is marked by a stone high up on the outside wall which you can see from the churchyard (reached along Seething Lane). Inside the church is a 19th-century memorial to Pepys high up on the north wall, the church authorities evidently bearing no grudge against a man who once wrote that he 'slept soundly all the sermon'. When Pepy's long-suffering wife died, her husband commissioned John Bushell, well known for his animated sculptures, to produce a fine white marble bust of her still to be found on the south wall, gazing over at her husband's memorial. Pepys was later buried beside her, underneath the communion table and just a mile from St Bride's where he was baptised.

The church retains other interesting features, despite severe damage incurred during the Blitz. The pulpit, reputedly carved by Grinling Gibbons, came from the 'lost' Wren church of St Benet Gracechurch Street, and St Olave's still has four fine 18th-century sword rests. The reredos in the Parish Chapel, on the left as you enter the church, was a gift from the Lloyd's Register of Shipping after the Second World War. To the left of the altar is a dramatic and colourful early 17th-century monument to the Bayninge brothers, Aldermen Andrew and Paul, both kneeling for deliverance. In the south aisle there is a beautifully carved marble monument to Sir James Deane (d. 1608) showing him at prayer alongside his three wives. The late 13th-century crypt, now a chapel, can also be visited. Given its dedication, it was appropriate that King Haakon VII of Norway laid the new foundation stone of St Olave's in 1951 and the careful restoration by Ernest Glanfield was completed in 1954. The entrance to the sanctuary is flanked by a stone mitre and the Norwegian crown. As you enter the churchyard off Seething Lane you are faced by the same formidable gates of 'St Ghastly Grim' that made a big impression on Charles Dickens. In the *Uncommercial Traveller* Dickens wrote of how he was 'once felt drawn to it in a thunderstorm at midnight. "Why not?" I said, in self-excuse, "I have been to the Colosseum by the light of the moon; is it worse to go and see St Ghastly Grim by the light of lightning?"'. Dickens described the 'gateway of St Ghastly Grim' as a '…small small

St Olave Hart Street

churchyard, with a ferocious strong piked iron gate, like a jail. This gate is ornamented with skulls and cross bones, larger than life wrought in stone.' The skull and crossbones are still very much in evidence, and this 1658 gateway, with its Latin inscription that translates as 'death is a light to me', is a forbidding sight if you approach on a dark winter's afternoon. In 1665 Mary Ramsey was buried here, who legend has it brought the Great Plague to London. The burial register also records a 'Mother Goose' who was buried here in 1586, perhaps the person who inspired the famous pantomime character of the same name?

Today the church continues to hold an annual Pepys Commemoration Service at the end of May and also serves as the church of the Clothworkers Company.

Hart Street, EC3; Nearest transport Tower Hill LU; Open Mon-Fri 9am-5pm

St Paul's Cathedral

38. St Paul's Cathedral

'Lector, Si monumentum requiris circumspice' (*'Reader, if you seek his monument, look around you'- epitaph from the tomb of Sir Christopher Wren*)

St Paul's, Wren's masterpiece, is of course different from his other City churches in being a 'cathedral', a term derived from the Greek word 'cathedra', meaning a seat or chair. In the Christian context this refers to the ceremonial bishop's throne found in each cathedral, the church that serves as the mother church to all others in a particular diocese. Each diocese has its own bishop and St Paul's is the cathedral for the Diocese of London.

Wren's building is the fifth on the site, the original having been founded in 604 AD by Mellitus, Bishop of the East Saxons. The first building burnt down and was rebuilt, but was later destroyed by the Vikings. It was subsequently rebuilt by the Saxons, and again by the Normans following a fire in 1087 – although this building was not actually consecrated until 1300. By the time of the English Civil War in the 17th century the cathedral was becoming increasingly dilapidated, and even before the Great Fire of 1666 gutted the Norman building, Wren had drawn up plans for its restoration. Following the Great Fire, Charles II commissioned Wren to rebuild the cathedral – a task that would take 35 years, during which Wren would work for five different monarchs.

Despite his royal patronage, Wren battled with the conservative church authorities who disliked his radical new plans. Wren, frustrated by the rejection of his first two designs, astutely produced a third which was approved by Charles II in 1675. The famous 'Warrant design' included a crucial clause giving Wren discretion to change the official plan as he saw fit. Hidden behind large construction screens that masked Wren's true intentions, St Paul's began to be rebuilt. The shape, reflecting the need for compromise, incorporated a ground plan based on the Latin cross shape so beloved by the church authorities, together with Wren's huge, and very un-English, dome. Wren's battles with the authorities never ceased, and by 1710 when the great cathedral was formally opened the old man had been side-lined – reduced to complaining to Queen Anne about how others had finished some minor aspects of his design.

Having famously survived the Second World War largely unscathed, the building we see today is much as it would have appeared to Wren. From its re-opening, St Paul's has served a crucial part in the life of London, hosting amongst many notable events the funerals of Lord Nelson (1806), the Duke of Wellington (1852), and Sir Winston Churchill (1965); the marriage of Charles, Prince of Wales, and Lady Diana Spencer (1981); and the Jubilee services of Queen Victoria (Diamond, 1897) and Queen Elizabeth II (Golden, 2002).

Outside the western entrance you will see a statue of Queen Anne (1665-1714), during whose reign the building was finished. The pediment of the famous portico, which has benefited from recent restoration work, contains a relief depicting the Conversion of St Paul, whilst above it stands the figure of the saint looking out over London, flanked by the figures of Saint James and Saint Peter. Inside the first impression is the huge scale of the building, the long nave of one of the world's largest cathedrals sweeping up to the famous dome ahead. The aisles of the nave are home to many of the finest of St Paul's 300 monuments to the great and the good of British history, the most impressive (found at the north end) being Alfred Steven's memorial to the Duke of Wellington, victor of Waterloo and later British Prime Minister. Just inside the entrance is a poignant floor memorial to the fire-fighters who helped save St Paul's from destruction during the Second World War. On the north aisle can be found St Dunstan's chapel and All Soul's chapel, with the chapel of St Michael and St George found on the south aisle.

The dome stands at the intersection of the cathedral's nave and transept and is one of the largest of its kind in the world weighing in at nearly 65,000 tonnes. The dome's murals date from the 18th century, whilst the surrounding mosaics are Victorian. You can visit the dome's galleries (entrance at the junction of the south transept and nave), the lowest being the interior Whispering Gallery, 259 steps up, and famous for allowing you to whisper against the wall and be heard by someone on the opposite side. Higher up are the exterior Stone Gallery, and Golden Gallery, which offer magnificent views of London. Back at ground level, Lord Nelson's monument and the Captain Scott memorial can be found in the south transept.

The 'quire' at the east end is where the choir and clergy sit during services. The Bishop's 'cathedra' (or throne) can be found on the south side, many of the furnishings nearby are by Wren's master woodcarver Grinling Gibbons. Behind the 20th-century high altar lies the American Memorial Chapel honouring American servicemen based in Britain who died in the Second World War. Henry Moore's sculpture *Mother and Child* is located on the north side. The south 'quire' aisle also contains a marble effigy of John Donne (d.1631) poet and once Dean of the cathedral. It is a rare survivor of the pre-Great Fire cathedral, you can even see some scorch marks on its base. The north transept contains William Holman Hunt's famous painting *The Light of the World*, dating from 1900 and one of two versions by the artist.

The crypt of St Paul's is equally fascinating, a place were burials took place from the 18th century right up until 1936. The south aisle of the east end contains Wren's tomb and nearby can be found the memorials and tombs of Henry Moore, Sir Joshua Reynolds, Sir Alexander Fleming and composer Sir Arthur Sullivan. The centre of the crypt, under the dome, contains the caskets of the Duke of Wellington and Lord Nelson. There are also memorials in the crypt to Florence Nightingale, Ivor Novello, William Blake and John Constable. The crypt also contains a café (open Mon-Sun), catering for the many thousands of visitors to the cathedral every day.

Ludgate Hill, EC4M; Telephone 020 7236 4128; Nearest transport Mansion House and St Paul's LU, Blackfriars LU/Rail; Open Mon-Sat 8.30 am-last admission 4pm; Admission adults £8, children (under 16) £3.50; sometimes shut at short notice for special services – check diary page on website www.stpauls.co.uk

St Peter upon Cornhill

39. St Peter upon Cornhill

Possible ancient foundations, first recorded early 11th century; restored in 1630s but destroyed in Great Fire; rebuilt by Wren; restored 19th century

Standing on the highest ground in the City, St Peter's has ancient foundations. A brass tablet inside claims the church was founded in 179 AD by King Lucius, a British king from the Roman period. However, this claim cannot be substantiated as their is little evidence of such a king – he is perhaps the result of erroneous research by the Anglo-Saxon chronicler Bede. Elizabethan historian John Stow refers to Lucius's original church being the pre-eminent place of worship in London until the arrival of St Augustine. It may well date from Saxon times when the crumbling Roman Forum was reoccupied. The church's claims of antiquity were once at the centre of a bitter 15th-century dispute between the parishioners of St Peter's, St Magnus' and St Nicholas Cole Abbey over whose rector should have precedence in religious celebrations. The matter was eventually decided in favour of St Peter's because of the general consensus it had the most ancient foundation. St Peter's had a grammar school and library in medieval times, something normally only found in cathedrals.

The importance of this church and the pre-eminent position of its rector helped it escape the controversial Victorian Union of Benefices Act that paved the way for the demolition of many other City churches. The medieval church was largely destroyed in the Great Fire and re-built by Wren in 1677-84 – possibly with Hooke's assistance. Further restorations were carried out in the 1880s and in 1990. It is not an easy church to gauge from the outside being mostly hidden behind office blocks – the best view is from Gracechurch Street where you can see the stuccoed east façade facing onto the street with the tower behind. Alternatively, walk down the tiny St Peter's Alley on the north side, where you come out into the churchyard and from where you can get a good look at the tower. The latter view would be similar to that seen by Charles

Dickens which he described in *A Mutual Friend* as 'a churchyard; a paved court, with a raised bank of earth about breast high, in the middle enclosed by iron rails.' The base of the tower is from the pre-Great Fire church and Wren chose to reconstruct the remains in a similar red brick style. The weather vane on top of the 140 feet tower symbolises St Peter's keys to the gates of heaven and there is also a figure of St Peter above the churchyard gate.

The interior is substantial, although it is no longer set up for regular services and appears a little tatty. It is now used as a Christian study centre. Most of the Wren furnishings, as with many of his other City churches, were removed by the Victorians and particularly by JD Wyatt in 1872. The church is, however, notable for containing one of only two remaining original Wren wooden chancel screens and the only one still in its original position. It is said that Wren was reluctant to have a screen at all, but the rector insisted and so Wren asked his teenage daughter to produce the design. The fine pulpit and sounding board survived the Victorian restoration, as did the Bernard Schmidt (or 'Father Smith') organ case – although this has been restored many times since being installed in 1681. Mendelssohn a true musical celebrity of his era, signed the keyboard when he played here on September 1st 1840 and declared the organ the 'finest in London'. The keyboard can now been seen, upon request, in the organ gallery. Below the organ gallery you can see the original 17th-century shelves that held bread for distribution to the poor. The font dates from the 17th century, whilst its carved cover is a rare survivor from the pre-Wren church.

The church has several military connections, most notably with The Royal Tank Regiment who use St Peter's as their regimental church. The stained glass on the north side commemorates the RTR, whilst other regiments are commemorated in windows on the south side. You may also notice that Wren's screen seems to be at a slight angle as a result of having to fit into a church whose east and west walls are not quite parallel. This is thought to be because all the various church buildings over the centuries including Wren's, were based upon the original imperfect Roman foundations. By the screen is a poignant memorial to the seven children of James and Mary Woodmason, who returned from a society ball at St James one night in 1782 to find their children dead from a fire.

Today, St Peter's is a Guild Church, run as a Christian study centre by the staff of St Helen's, so there are no regular public services. As can be seen below, the fine ceiling and surrounding decoration are let down by the furniture that now occupies the central space.

Cornhill EC3; Nearest transport Bank LU; Not normally open to public, call St Helen's, 020 7283 2231

40. St Sepulchre without Newgate

First recorded 1137; rebuilt mid 15th century but gutted in Great Fire; repaired by parishioners; rebuilt in 19th and 20th centuries; damaged in Blitz

More formally known as the 'Church of the Holy Sepulchre without Newgate', this church was originally dedicated to St Edmund. Its location outside the north-west gate of the City, just like the famous St Sepulchre in Jerusalem, resulted in it becoming a symbolic departure point for medieval Crusaders and so the dedication was officially changed during the 15th century. The porch, tower and outer walls date from about 1450, however the main body of the church was destroyed during the Great Fire. Today's building is essentially a reconstruction dating from 1667-71, commissioned by parishioners too impatient to wait for Wren to start work. They instead employed one of his master masons Joshua Marshall. The current interior layout dates from 1875 with further reordering in 1932 by Sir Charles Nicholson. The lofty roof and plaster ceilings date from the early 19th century. The result is not the most elegant of City churches, with the cumulative work over the centuries resembling a jumble of various architectural styles.

Lying outside the old City wall, this was a large parish less constrained by available land and as a result St Sepulchre's is one of the biggest City churches. The church had a strong association with the infamous Newgate prison that stood opposite on the site of the current Old Bailey. Newgate was an important place in London life from medieval times onwards, with many well-known figures imprisoned there including Titus Oates, William Penn and Daniel Defoe. The church was once connected to Newgate by a tunnel and parishioner Robert Dowe left £50 in 1605 for a man to ring a handbell and say a prayer at midnight for those prisoners due to be executed the following day. The grisly prayer and ringing of the bell must have added greatly to the condemned man's fears, especially as the last few words were shouted through the keyhole of the prisoner's cell. The handbell is housed today in a glass case at the south-east end of the nave. The church bells were also rung to mark the time of executions and prisoners were given flowers at the church gates on their way to the gallows at Tyburn or Smithfield. After public executions were moved from Tyburn to Newgate in the late 18th century, the area outside the church would have been thronged on execution days with people struggling to obtain the best vantage point.

Unsurprisingly, St Sepulchre's ominous bells were well known to Londoners. Dickens refers to them in both *Barnaby Rudge* and *Oliver Twist*. They are also mentioned in the famous children's rhyme 'Oranges and Lemons', 'When will you pay me, Say the bells of Old Bailey'. The imposing 150 feet tower contains a ring of 12 bells, most of which were made in 1739, replacing those originally bought from St Bartholomew the Great in 1537. On the north side of the church facing Giltspur Street is a post-Second World War reconstruction of the original late 18th-century Watch House. It was from here that churchwardens would guard against body-snatchers taking dead parishioners back to the surgeons of St Bartholomew's Hospital for illegal medical examinations.

St Sepulchre's is notable for being the Musicians' Church. The north chapel was converted into the Musicians Chapel in 1955 and there are frequent lunchtime recitals. Sir Henry Wood (1869-1944), conductor and co-founder of London's famous Promenade Concerts, was christened here, and became assistant organist aged 14. The chapel has stained glass windows commemorating Wood, and also composer John Ireland and Australian singer Dame Nellie Melba. On the Last Night of the Proms at the Albert Hall a wreath is placed on the bust of Sir Henry then brought here the next day to be placed with his ashes inside the church.

The south chapel is dedicated to the City of London Regiment of the Royal Fusiliers and featured in a scene from *The Wall* – a film inspired by Pink Floyd and starring Bob Geldof. Captain John Smith, the Governor of Virginia famous for being saved by the American Indian Princess Pocahontas, was buried here in 1631 and before his death lived nearby in a house on Snow Hill. A brass plaque to Smith on the south-east end remembers that 'Here lyes one conquered, that hath conquered Kings, Subdu'd large Territories, and done Things Which to the world impossible would seem'.

A large window on the south end from 1968 depicts Smith holding a map of Virginia. Former rector John Rogers, who helped Tyndale translate the Bible into English, became the first Protestant martyr of Queen Mary's reign. He was burnt at the stake in nearby Smithfield in 1555.

Holborn Viaduct, EC1; Nearest transport St Paul's and Chancery Lane LU; Open Wed 11am-3pm and Thursday lunchtime recitals

St Sepulchre

41. St Stephen Walbrook

Saxon origins, first recorded late 11th century; rebuilt 15th century; destroyed in Great Fire; rebuilt by Wren, damaged in Blitz; reordered 1980s

With the exception of St Paul's, St Stephen Walbrook is often regarded as Wren's greatest City church, although to some its clean lines are less attractive than the more atmospheric St Mary Abchurch nearby. The original building was Saxon, possibly built as early as the 8th century. Dedicated to the first Christian martyr, it was first recorded when William the Conqueror's steward donated the church to Colchester Abbey in 1096. The church stood on the east bank of the Wall Brook stream whose course is now hidden under the road. The church was later rebuilt around 1430 on the west bank of the stream, but then destroyed in the Great Fire. Rebuilt by Wren in 1672-80, it was one of his earliest, and largest City churches. The pains taken with the church are perhaps partly explained by the fact that Wren used to live next door.

The modest exterior, comprising a square ragstone tower and steeple and almost invisible green Byzantine style dome, contrast with the fantastic interior. This is reached after trudging up steep steps, past a stone tablet on the wall with a Latin inscription praising Wren, and on under a baroque screen beneath the organ case. Once inside, the church feels bright and intimate, crowned by a glorious dome that was the first of its kind in any English church – a forerunner of Wren's work on St Paul's Cathedral. In fact, this dome is different in that the inside and outside are the same except for the thickness of materials, whereas the dome of St Paul's is supported by timbers and a ceiling of a different shape. It is not known whether Mr Pollixifen, who lived beside the church and complained bitterly that Wren's building was reducing the light to his property, was ever placated once he was able to see what his antagonist had achieved. Certainly the rest of Europe was impressed. The sculptor Antonio Canova (of 'The Three Graces' fame) expressed a desire to visit London merely to see St Paul's, Somerset House and St Stephen Walbrook.

The beautifully lit interior is in the shape of a Latin cross. The almost circular dome is carried on eight arches and freestanding columns, giving the appearance of a building within a building. After being damaged in the Blitz, the church was successfully restored by Godfrey Allen 1951-2. In the following years water from the stream below caused further destruction and the church was controversially re-ordered under the sponsorship of Lord Palumbo between 1978-87. This explains the striking ten tonne Travertine altar in the middle of the floor that was carved by Henry Moore in a quarry near Rome once used by Michelangelo. The altar, once compared to a 'ripe camembert cheese', sat redundant in a field near Moore's studio while its controversial installation was considered at a sitting of the Court of Ecclesiastical Causes Reserved. The reredos give an indication of where the old altar would have been before the re-ordering.

There are many interesting memorials including a modern one to John Dunstable, a master of astronomy once described as 'the greatest composer in Europe', who was buried in the old church in 1453. There is also a memorial to Dr Nathaniel Hodges, buried here in 1688, who bravely stayed in London during the Great Plague of 1665 to help the sick. Sir John Vanbrugh, playwright and architect of Blenheim Palace (d. 1726), was also buried here. The telephone in a glass box found on the west end was used by rector Dr Chad Varah in 1952 as a helpline for those in need, a service that developed into the hugely important Samaritans organisation. Today, there is no more splendid place in the City to listen to one of the many lunchtime musical recitals.

Walbrook, EC4; Nearest transport Bank LU; Open Mon-Fri 10am-4pm (3pm on Fri)

St Stephen Walbrook

St Vedast alias Foster

42. St Vedast alias Foster

Founded possibly 12th century; rebuilt 16th and early 17th centuries; destroyed by Great Fire and rebuilt by Wren; gutted in Blitz and restored 1962

Dedicated to the Bishop of Arras who died in 540 AD, St Vedast's is traditionally claimed to have been established by 1170. In this country the name has changed over the years from St Vedast (or St Vaast in Arras), to Vastes, Fastes, Faster, Fauster and then finally to Foster. The first official record of this church however dates from the 13th century when it may have been used by a local Flemish community of artisans. In medieval times the church was one of 13 under the Archbishop of Canterbury's jurisdiction in the City of London, a situation that continued until the 19th century. Poet Robert Herrick (d.1674), disciple of Ben Jonson, and son of a London goldsmith, was baptized in the old church in 1591. The Great Fire destroyed the old church, although the base of the tower and the lower walls survived. After the fire, the building was hastily repaired although it was soon rebuilt by Wren between 1695–1712. The distinctively simple 160 feet tower, said to have been designed to contrast with the elaborate tower of nearby St Mary le Bow, has been attributed by some to Wren's assistant Nicholas Hawksmoor. Wren's church incorporated the remains of the pre-Fire building and followed the same plan. Within the irregular medieval plan Wren created an illusion of regularity in a new, classically inspired design using high quality plasterwork and woodwork. Recent cleaning on the south side has revealed older features which remain unaltered from before the Great Fire.

Wren's church survived largely intact until being gutted during the Blitz with only the walls, tower and steeple surviving. Post-war restoration was completed in 1962 by Stephen Dykes Bower in a design sympathetic to Wren's original. High quality furnishings were taken from 'lost' City churches such as the reredos from St Christopher le Stocks, the altar table from St Matthew Friday Street, the organ case from St Bartholomew by the Exchange, and the elegantly carved pulpit from All Hallows Bread Street. The architect also introduced a collegiate seating pattern and modern glass by Brian Thomas.

Standing on the street it is easy to look inside the church through the recently added glass doors. The interior of this modestly sized church contains a font, still in regular use, which dates from the late 17th century. It was originally made for St Anne and St Agnes nearby and is said to be the work of Grinling Gibbons. The reredos behind the modern altar is thought to date from the 17th century, and comprises three panels with the *Ten Commandments* in the middle, the *Our Father* and the *Apostles' Creed* on either side. The small chapel on the right of the altar is dedicated jointly to Our Lady and to St Dunstan, the Goldsmiths Company's patron saint. The dedication to St Dunstan, himself a skilled goldsmith, originated because of the church's links with the Goldsmiths Company nearby, possibly another indication that St Vedast may have been linked to an early medieval Flemish artisan community. The altar includes pieces that came from All Hallows Bread Street.

In the churchyard there is an interesting memorial erected by George Courtauld and other friends with the epitaph, 'In memory of "Petro", Major Vladimir Vassilievitch Petropavlovsky 1888-1971, Soldier of the Tsar – of France – of England. This was a Man.'

Foster Lane, Cheapside EC2; Nearest transport St Paul's LU; Open Mon-Fri 7.30am-6pm

St Vedast alias Foster

43. Temple Church

Founded 12th century; survived Great Fire but rebuilt by
Wren; reconstructed 1841; gutted in Blitz; reopened 1958

The Temple Church of St Mary is well-hidden amongst the maze
of barristers' chambers that forms the Inner and Middle Temple.
You can find the church by following a small alley on the south side
of Fleet Street nearly opposite St Dunstan in the West. The church
was famously founded by the Knights Templar, an order of monks
established in Jerusalem following the First Crusade to protect pilgrims travelling to the Holy Land. Their original base was on the
site of Solomon's Temple, but they quickly spread throughout
medieval Europe, becoming hugely influential in the process. The
Master of the Temple in England even sat in Parliament as the first
baron of the realm ('primus baro Angiae'). Following the loss of the
Holy Land to the Saracens and the growing hostility of the Papacy
and medieval monarchs, the Templars became increasingly vulnera-
ble. Philip IV of France and the Pope instituted a Europe wide persecution of the Templars in the early 14th century causing the col-
lapse of the order.

The Templars modelled their churches on the circular Holy
Sepulchre in Jerusalem, said to have been the site of the tomb of
Christ. Temple Church was part of a grander Templar base following the move of the Order from High Holborn and was probably
used even before the consecration in 1185 by Heraclius, Patriarch
of Jerusalem, in the presence of King Henry II. Such was the influence of the Templars that Henry III professed a wish to be buried
in the church and a large choir was built in anticipation. Whilst the
King (d.1272) attended the subsequent consecration, he later
changed his mind and was instead buried in Westminster Abbey.
After the suppression of the Templars, the church fell into the hands
of Edward II who gave it to another military/religious order, the
Knights Hospitaller. This order rented the building out to lawyers
whose chambers became known as the Inner and Middle Temple.
When the Hospitallers were abolished by Henry VIII the building

Temple Church

became a 'royal peculiar', meaning it came under the direct control of the King who appointed the priest known as 'Master of the Temple'. In 1608 James I granted a Royal Charter so the two Inns of Court could use the Temple provided they paid for the upkeep and the two colleges of barristers share the church to this day.

Although the church survived the Great Fire, it was nevertheless restored by Wren, and heavily restored once more in 1841 in a Victorian Gothic style. The Blitz gutted the building, including the wooden furnishings, and it was reconstructed by Walter and Emil Godfrey in the 1950s. Luckily the original Wren reredos was restored having been kept in a museum by the Victorians.

The church has often been at the centre of controversy. In 1585 the second Master died and his deputy Walter Travers was passed over for promotion because of his Calvinist views. Richard Hooker was appointed instead, but Travers took his revenge. Whilst Hooker would preach on Sunday mornings, Travers would contradict his rival in his own afternoon sermon. This became known as the 'Battle of the Pulpit'. Hooker later published *Ecclesiastical Polity* and became known as a founding father of Anglican theology.

After the Great Fire the two Inns of Court could not agree on whether to commission an organ made by Bernard Schmidt ('Father Smith') or Renatus Harris, the two greatest organ makers of their era and bitter rivals. A bad-tempered dispute broke out with musical trials taking place that included a performance by court composer George Frederick Handel. The decision for Father Smith was made by 'Hanging' Judge Jeffreys, more famous for his involvement in the 'Bloody Assizes' than his musical ear. The winning organ continued to be used until it was destroyed during the Blitz.

The church is formed of two parts, the Round and the Rectangular Chancel. The Round Church contains some striking 12th and 13th-century life-sized stone effigies of medieval knights that were laid out here during the 1841 restoration. Most display crossed legs that signify their Crusader status. The most famous effigy is that of Crusader William the Marshal, Earl of Pembroke (d.1219), an important mediator between King John and the Barons in 1215. As a young man he was a hugely famous and undefeated fighter in martial tournaments. Pembroke's eldest son, also William (d.1231), was chosen by the barons to help force King John to comply with the Magna Carta, and his effigy lies next to his father's. Another effigy is that of the East Anglian magnate, Geoffrey de Mandeville (d.1144).

Today the church is sought out by tourists fascinated by the part it plays in Dan Brown's international best seller *The Da Vinci Code*. It seems the public fascination with the mystical Templar Order will continue to ensure this is one of the most popular City churches. The church also has a very active programme of musical recitals and is frequently used for marriages and baptisms by the barristers who work in the vicinity.

Temple, EC4 (off Fleet Street); Nearest transport Chancery Lane and Temple LU, Blackfriars LU/Rail; Open Wed-Sun 10am-4pm

WILLIAM MARSHAL
Earl of Pembroke died...

Temple Church

The Spanish and Potuguese Synagogue

44. The Spanish and Portuguese Synagogue
Opened 1701

Built for Sephardic worship at the beginning of the 18th century, this building is important for being the oldest surviving synagogue in England. The Jews were expelled from England in 1290, however under Cromwell's Commonwealth they were permitted to settle here once more. The first Jewish place of worship was originally founded in the mid 17th century in nearby Creechurch Lane, but the growing congregation required a larger building. In 1701 the current structure was opened and has remained largely unaltered since that time. The plain exterior is tucked away behind a small courtyard off Bevis Marks, a reminder of the days when Jews were forbidden to build on busy streets. The interior is therefore a delightful surprise – both elegant and opulent in equal measure and similar in many ways to Christian buildings constructed during the same period. This may be explained partly because of the involvement of Quaker carpenter Joseph Avis in the design and construction and much of the woodwork was crafted by men who worked with Wren. The seven candelabra symbolise the seven days of the week, and add to the light within this simple oblong building. The 12 Tuscan columns support the galleries on three sides representing the 12 tribes of Israel, whilst the two-storied Ark with Corinthian columns houses the Torah scrolls. The overall arrangement has been compared to the Great Synagogue at Amsterdam built in 1675.

The 19th-century Prime Minister and author Benjamin Disraeli is recorded in the Register of Births, however his parents fell out with the Synagogue and he was later baptised as a Christian in St Andrew Holborn. Jacob Sasporta (1610-1698) was once chief rabbi and was prominent in denouncing the teachings of Shabbetai Zvi, a 'false messiah' who threatened the global foundations of the Jewish faith in the 17th century. Legendary 19th century pugilist David Mendoza (1763-1836) also worshiped here.

Bevis Marks, EC3; Nearest transport Aldgate LU; Open Mon, Tues, Wed and Fri 11am-1pm, Sun 11am-12.30pm

45. The City Temple (United Reformed Church)
Built 1870s; gutted in Blitz, reopened 1958

When it was built in 1873-74 at the cost of £35,000 under the sponsorship of minister Joseph Parker this was the second largest Nonconformist chapel in London. The congregation had obviously prospered since their mid 17th-century origins when non-conformists had no permanent places of worship. The huge central hall is capable of holding 2,500 people and the rest of the building contains many other rooms and facilities. The substantial Italian influenced façade of Bath stone facing onto Holborn Viaduct is largely original, however the interior is very modern following major restoration undertaken in 1955-58 after the building had been gutted in the Blitz. This has resulted in the great hall having an appearance similar to a large university lecture theatre.

Holborn Viaduct, EC1; Nearest transport Chancery Lane LU (closed Sunday); Open Mon-Fri 8am-6pm

46. Jewin Welsh Presbyterian Church
Built 1879, destroyed in Blitz; rebuilt and reopened 1961

In the 18th century many Welsh people came to London to seek work and c.1774 some would meet to hold a service in a pub in Cock Lane, Smithfield. Later a chapel was built on Jewin Crescent, once the site of a burial ground granted to the Jews in 1177, hence the name. However the growing congregation resulted in the construction of a larger chapel in 1878-79 by Charles Bell located in Fann Street near the Barbican estate. This chapel was destroyed during the Blitz and rebuilt in an English version of Modernism known as 'New Humanism' by Caroe and Partners. The foundation stone was laid in 1960 and the plain brick rectangular building was reopened the following year, largely due to the energetic efforts of Reverend D. Owen (d.1959). Services are held each Sunday, although to a dwindling congregation.

Fann Street, EC1; Nearest transport Barbican LU/Rail; Contact church for visiting arrangements telephone 0207 628 8370

47. St Mary Aldermanbury

First recorded 1181; destroyed in Great Fire and rebuilt by Wren 1671-75; destroyed in Blitz, moved to Fulton, Missouri, USA in 1965

Just north of the Guildhall Library can be found a small garden built around the remains of St Mary Aldermanbury. In the garden is a bust of Shakespeare and memorial to two of his fellow actors, John Heminges and Henry Condell. Heminges and Condell lived in the parish and were buried in the old churchyard. It was through their efforts that Shakespeare's works were collected and printed in 1623 for the first time in what is known as the First Folio. The medieval church was destroyed in the Great Fire and rebuilt by Wren. Soon after, the body of the infamous Judge George Jeffreys was reburied here three years after he had died in the Tower in 1689. Jeffreys was known as the 'Hanging Judge' after his vicious trials of captured rebels in the West Country became known as the Bloody Assizes.

The church was gutted in the Blitz, however whilst it was not rebuilt after the Second World War something rather extraordinary did happen to it. In 1965 its 7,000 Portland stones were moved to the USA and reconstructed by architect Eris Lytle on the campus of Westminster College in Fulton, Missouri. This amazing project commemorated Winston Churchill's visit to the College in 1946 when he referred in his speech to the 'Iron Curtain' and the 'special relationship' between Britain and the US – phrases that almost immediately passed into general usage.

Towers

a. All Hallows Staining

Opposite Fenchurch Street Station, a short stone tower is all that remains of the 15th-century church. 'Staining' means 'made of stone', perhaps used to distinguish it from other churches named All Hallows that stood in the City. The medieval church survived the Great Fire but largely collapsed in 1671 because excessive burials had weakened its foundations. The rebuilt church was later pulled down in 1870, leaving only the tower. The 15th-century church bell ended up in Grocers' Hall and is the oldest bell in the City. It is said that Elizabeth I visited the church after her release from the Tower nearby, making a present of new bell-ropes because in captivity All Hallows' bells had been 'music to her ears'.

Star Alley, Mark Lane EC3; Nearest transport Tower Hill LU

b. Christ Church Newgate

The original church was built in the early 14th century by the Franciscans as part of Greyfriars Monastery. At 300 feet long it was the largest church in London aside from St Paul's, its eminence such that four queens are known to have been buried there. However its glory days ended with Henry VIII's Dissolution of the Monasteries, when Greyfriars was used for storing war spoils among other things. Part of the Greyfriars building became the church of a newly created parish and was renamed Christchurch. It also housed Christ's Hospital, a school for 'poor fatherless children', until the school moved to Horsham, Sussex in 1897. The church itself was destroyed in the Great Fire, and Wren's replacement, at 113 feet, was much smaller. The Blitz destroyed the Wren church and today only the substantial steeple formed of triple-tiered squares remains in addition to some walls and a garden within the former nave.

King Edward Street, EC1; Nearest transport St Paul's LU

c. St Alban Wood Street

It is believed that Offa, King of Mercia (d.796), once had a palace and chapel on this site. Offa founded St Albans Abbey and the dedication to this saint was popular in Saxon times. The medieval church, said to have been rebuilt under Inigo Jones in the 1630s, was destroyed in the Great Fire. It was rebuilt by Wren in the 1680s, then destroyed in the Blitz. The remaining walls came down in 1954 and today only the elegant Wren tower remains.
Wood Street, EC2; Nearest transport St Paul's LU

d. St Augustine with St Faith

Situated a stone's throw to the east of St Paul's, the original church was first recorded in the mid 12th century. It was destroyed in the Great Fire and rebuilt by Wren in 1680-83, with a later tower perhaps by Nicholas Hawksmoor. After further changes in the 19th century, the church was destroyed in the Blitz and only the tower remains. This has been incorporated into the modernist building of St Paul's Cathedral Choir School. During the Second World War, the church housed a famous cat named Faith. Originally a stray, Faith lived in the Rectory beside the church. One night in September 1940 Faith courageously saved her kittens from the Blitz and earned a unique wartime decoration.
Watling Street, EC4; Nearest transport St Paul's LU

e. St Dunstan in the East

Originating in the 13th century and dedicated to a Saxon Archbishop of Canterbury, this church largely survived the Great Fire however Wren rebuilt the tower and steeple. This may explain why he used an uncharacteristically Gothic design in keeping with the existing structure and it is said his daughter Jane helped in the design. It is also said that Wren had such confidence in its construction that when told the steeple of every City church had been damaged in a hurricane that hit London in 1703, he replied 'Not St Dunstan's, I am sure'. Sadly the church did not survive the Blitz,

only the tower and shell of the nave remains. However, of all the remaining towers this is the most beautiful, and the garden within the shell is one of the most pleasant in the City.
Idol Lane, London EC3; Nearest transport Monument LU

f. St Martin Orgar

The original church was first mentioned in the 12th century. It was destroyed except for the tower and part of the nave in the Great Fire. Members of the congregation moved to St Clement's instead, although French Protestants decided to restore the tower and worshipped in it until it was demolished in 1820. The current Italianate tower dates from 1852 and was used as a rectory by St Clement's.
Martin Lane, EC3; Nearest transport Monument LU

g. St Mary Somerset

First mentioned in 1170, the medieval church was destroyed in the Great Fire and rebuilt by Wren. The 17th-century Bishop and vice chancellor of Oxford University Gilbert Ironside was buried here. He is best remembered for bravely defending the rights of his fellow academics against the intrusions of James II. The church was destroyed under the Victorian Union of Benefices Act leaving just Wren's tower remaining.
Upper Thames Street, EC4; Nearest transport Mansion House LU or Blackfriars Rail LU/Rail

h. St Olave Jewry

First mentioned in the late 12th century, the medieval church was destroyed in the Great Fire and rebuilt by Wren in 1676. It was later demolished by the Victorians in 1888, leaving just the tower and a pretty garden. The proceeds from the sale went towards building a new St Olave's in the expanding suburbs at Manor Park. Today the tower forms part of a City office.
Ironmonger Lane, EC2; Nearest transport Bank LU

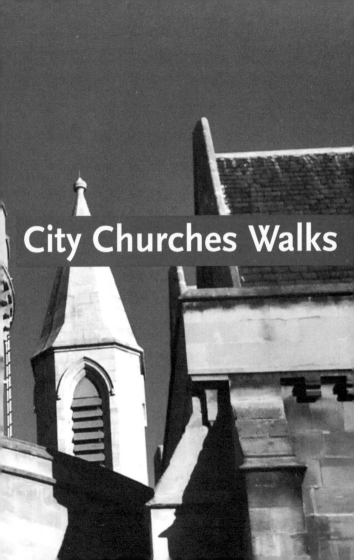

City Churches Walks

Eastern Walk

Walk begins at Liverpool Street Station and ends at Monument
Nearest transport Liverpool Station LU and Rail

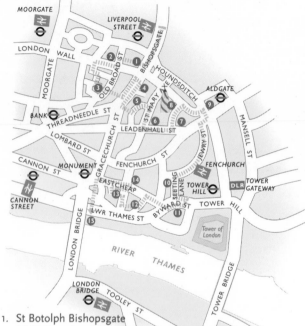

1. St Botolph Bishopsgate
2. All Hallows London Wall
3. Dutch Church Austin Friars
4. St Ethelburga the Virgin
5. St Helen Bishopsgate
6. St Andrew Undershaft
7. St Katherine Cree
8. Spanish & Portuguese
    Synagogue

9. St Botolph Aldgate
10. St Olave Hart Street
11. All Hallows by the Tower
12. St Dunstan in the East
13. St Mary at Hill
14. St Margaret Pattens
15. St Magnus the Martyr

Stand at the exit of Liverpool Street that faces onto Bishopsgate then turn right (south) for a 100 metres or so until you reach **(1) St Botolph Bishopsgate** (see page 57), a largely 18th-century church designed by James Gold and set in a lovely garden that was once controversial for being the first City churchyard to be converted for such a purpose in the 1860s. When finished at the church, walk through the garden past the former charity school on the right, and netball court on the left, and continue straight ahead. You will pass a distinctive and tiny Italian restaurant, formerly a

Turkish bath. When you reach Old Broad Street turn left until you reach London Wall and then head right along London Wall and you will soon see on your right the back of the plain brick wall of **(2) All Hallows** (see page 21). This is a mainly 18th-century church elegantly designed by George Dance the Younger and which today houses several charities.

When leaving All Hallows cross over London Wall and walk down the left hand side heading west until you take the first left at Great Winchester Street. Continue down this street until you see a small alleyway (Austin Friars Passage) on the right hand side which brings you out onto Austin Friars Square and the **(3) Dutch Church Austin Friars** (see page 72). The Dutch Church, as its name suggests, is still used by a Dutch congregation for services, their links with this church beginning in the 16th century. Van Gogh sketched the old church in the 19th century whilst living in Brixton.

On leaving the Dutch Church, walk east along Pinners Passage (to your left as you exit the alley onto the square) which takes you back onto Old Broad Street. Immediately opposite you will see Tower 42 (formerly the NatWest Tower) – still the tallest building in the City. Cross over the road and proceed down the path that leads immediately left of Tower 42 until you walk onto Bishopsgate itself.

Immediately opposite on the other side of Bishopsgate is the entrance to Great St Helen's where St Helen's church is found. Before visiting, cross over Bishopsgate and bear left for about 50 metres until you reach the front of **(4) St Ethelburga's** (see page 77). This is the smallest church in the City and until being largely destroyed by an IRA bomb in the early 90s was perhaps the best surviving example of a medieval church in the Square Mile. It now houses The Centre for Peace and Reconciliation – be sure to visit the tranquil memorial garden at the rear (down a small alley way on the left).

From St Ethelburga's retrace your steps along Bishopsgate until you reach the entrance for Great St Helen's on the left, and take it to find **(5) St Helen's** (see page 83), part of the parish where Shakespeare once lived. St Helen's is known as the 'Westminster Abbey' of the City for the number of fine monuments inside its walls. On the outside of the building you can see where the church of the medieval nunnery joined the once separate parish church. The buildings were amalgamated after the Dissolution of the Monasteries.

When leaving St Helen's walk by the side of the church along Undershaft directly towards the base of the huge 'cigar' of the Swiss Re building directly ahead on St Mary Axe. At this road turn right and walk south to the junction with Leadenhall Street. You will see

the famous Lloyd's Insurance building on the other side of Leadenhall Street, while on the left at the junction with Leadenhall Street you will find **(6) St Andrew Undershaft** (see page 29). St Andrew's is not normally open to visitors, however its interior contains the fine tomb of Elizabethan John Stow whose Survey of London was an important record of the City as it then was.

Leave St Andrew's and turn left down Leadenhall Street until you reach **(7) St Katherine Cree** (see page 91) after about 100 metres on the left hand side. St Katherine's was built in the 1630s and is particularly notable for being a rare example of church architecture from this period. It also contains a fine 16th-century monument to Sir Nicholas Throckmorton. When you leave St Katherine's turn immediately right and right again down Creechurch Lane

alongside the church and walk down the lane until you reach Bevis Marks (about 150 metres). Turn left on Bevis Marks and after about 25 metres on your left you will find the **(8) Spanish and Portuguese Synagogue** (see page 165), a very important early City synagogue built in the 17th century after Cromwell allowed the Jews to return to England.

When leaving the synagogue turn right back down Bevis Marks and continue walking straight on (past Creechurch Lane). You should shortly see about 200 metres away the spire of **(9) St Botolph Aldgate** (see page 53). Cross over at the junction to reach the church, which is one of three remaining City churches dedicat-ed to the patron saint of travellers – all of which

stood by major gates in the City wall (in this case Ald Gate). This church is heavily involved in helping the homeless of the area, and was described by Sir John Betjeman as 'more a mission to the East End than City church'.

When leaving St Botolph's, the next stop is a slightly longer walk to St Olave Hart Street, found by crossing over the road immediately outside the entrance to St Botolph's, then walking right until reach-ing Jewry Street. Walk along this street as it bends round, until it leads onto Crutched Friars – named after the monks who had an

abbey nearby until the Dissolution of the Monasteries. The figures of two Crutched Friars can be seen on your right as you walk down this road. Crutched Friars leads under the railway bridge (right hand fork) and after about 100 metres you reach Hart Street where you will see on the left the 'country church' of **(10) St Olave's** (see page 139). This is a small, but history-packed church that was attended by diarist Samuel Pepys and his wife when they lived nearby on Seething Lane. When leaving St Olave's head south down Seething Lane, stopping to visit the famous churchyard on the right hand side. The skulls above the entrance of 'St Ghastly Grim' made a big

impression on Charles Dickens who wrote of them in the *Uncommerical Traveller*. Also look to the left hand side of Seething Lane to a small garden that contains a bust and memorial to Pepys, marking the spot of the Navy Office where the diarist once worked and lived.

Continue down Seething Lane until you reach busy Byward Street, with **(11) All Hallows by the Tower** (see page 17) visible immediately across the road. Cross over (via the subway) and visit this church, making sure you see the undercroft with its fascinating museum of artefacts that prove this is one of the oldest City churches, having Saxon foundations.

When leaving All Hallows turn left and cross over immediately at the traffic lights so you cross over Byward Street and walk west down Great Tower Street. After about 100 metres on the left hand side turn left down St Dunstan's Hill until you see the back of the beautiful ruins of **(12) St Dunstan in the East** (see page 170), which contains perhaps the prettiest garden in the City. Wren's distinctive tower still stands, although the church itself was gutted in the Blitz and not rebuilt. Walk towards the base of the tower which faces onto Idol Lane and turn onto St Dunstan's Lane opposite the church. From here continue right along the Lane until you reach St Mary at Hill street.

Turn up this street and almost immediately on your left there is a small stone passageway. Beyond this can be seen the rear of the church of St Mary at Hill. Walk up this tiny passageway (just under the projecting church clock) until you reach Lovat Lane and turn immediately right until you reach the entrance of **(13) St Mary at Hill** (see page 122). This is a pretty Wren church that is slowly  being refurbished after suffering a terrible fire in 1988. Thomas á Becket is said to have been one of the medieval rectors here.

When leaving St Mary's turn right, continuing up the hill of Lovat Lane until you reach Eastcheap at the top. From here visit Wren's **(14) (St Margaret Pattens** see page 105), whose spire is just visible on the other side of the road on the right. Named after the 'pattenmakers' who built shoes for medieval Londoners, St Margaret's has the third highest parish church spire in the City.

When leaving St Margaret's retrace your steps and walk west along Eastcheap following the signs for Monument. Monument marks the spot where the Great Fire broke out in Pudding Lane in 1666. At Monument walk south down Fish Street Hill until you see the church of **(15) St Magnus the Martyr** (see page 99) directly across busy Lower Thames Street. St Magnus once stood on the entrance to old London Bridge, and is mentioned in TS Eliot's *The Waste Land*. St Magnus' is the last of the 15 churches featured in the Eastern Walk. If you still have the energy, retrace your steps and visit the Monument, the top of which offers incredible views of the City.

Middle Walk [Circular from Monument]
The walk begins at St Clement's, nearest transport Monument LU

1. St Clement Eastcheap
2. St Edmund King & Martyr
3. St Michael Cornhill
4. St Peter upon Cornhill
5. St Margaret Lothbury
6. St Lawrence Jewry
7. St Mary Aldermanbury
8. St Giles Cripplegate

9. St Alban Wood Street
10. St Mary le Bow
11. St Mary Aldermary
12. St James Garlickhythe
13. St Michael Paternoster Royal
14. St Stephen Walbrook
15. St Mary Woolnoth
16. St Mary Abchurch

Begin by walking up King William Street from Monument and almost immediately on your right is the tiny Clement's Lane. Walk up this lane and visit **(1) St Clement Eastcheap** (see page 65) almost immediately on your right. This Wren church is probably the one referred to in the nursery rhyme *Oranges and Lemons*. It now contains some interesting second-hand book stalls. When leaving St Clement's continue up the Lane until reaching Lombard Street. Here you will see the church of **(2) St Edmund King and Martyr** (see page 75) with its distinctive lead steeple and projecting clock directly ahead. St Edmund's now houses The London Centre for Spirituality.

Outside St Edmund's walk down George Yard alongside the church, continuing straight ahead down the tiny St Michael's Alley, past the Jamaica Wine House, until you reach Cornhill. At the junction with Cornhill on your right you will find **(3) St Michael Cornhill** (see page 129), a good example of a Victorian re-ordered City church and famous for the high standard of its music.

When leaving St Michael's continue right along Cornhill for 50 metres or so until you reach St Peter's Alley on the right hand side. Walk down this alley until you come out onto the open space opposite **(4) St Peter upon Cornhill** (see page 147). St Peter's is not normally open to the public, which is a pity because it houses one of only two Wren chancel screens in the City and the only one that is in its original position. St Peter's also claims to be the oldest City church with a plaque dating its origins to AD 179.

When finished, return onto Cornhill, then turn left and retrace your steps until you see Finch Lane on the other side of the street. Walk down Finch Lane until you reach Threadneedle Street where the Bank of England is based. Take a left at Threadneedle Street and then crossover to take Bartholomew Lane on the right and follow the Lane down alongside the Bank of England, until you reach Lothbury. At Lothbury turn left to see Wren's church of **(5) St Margaret Lothbury** (see page 102) on the other side of the street. St Margaret's is the only other City church that contains a Wren chancel screen. It is known as the 'banker's church' because of its proximity to the Bank of England.

When leaving St Margaret's continue along Lothbury over the junction, soon after which Lothbury becomes Gresham Street. The street is named after City grandee Sir Thomas Gresham, founder of Gresham College and The Royal Exchange, whose tomb can be found in St Helen's. About 100 metres after the junction on the right along Gresham Street you will find Wren's **(6) St Lawrence Jewry** (see page 95) and also Guildhall (home of the Corporation of London). Both buildings were built on the site of a 7,000 seat Roman amphitheatre.

When leaving St Lawrence bear right away from Gresham Street down Aldermanbury, and past the Guildhall Library where nearly all the parish records of the City churches are kept. At the end of this street stop to look at the small garden that marks the site of **(7) St Mary Aldermanbury** (see page 168), destroyed in the Blitz and rebuilt on the campus of Westminster College in Fulton, Missouri, USA. The garden contains a bust of Shakespeare and a monument to John Heminges and Henry Condell. Heminges and Condell were part of Shakespeare's acting company and were important in organising the first printing of his works.

With your back to the garden you will see on your right Love Lane, once a red light area in medieval times. Follow this Lane onto Wood Street and turn right at Wood Street (past the Wren tower of St Alban Wood Street). Head for the escalator on the left hand corner and go up onto the Barbican highwalk. At the top of the escalator walk between the two Pizza Express restaurants and continue straight ahead following the signs for the

Barbican Centre. After about 150 metres you will see an open space on your left and **(8) St Giles Cripplegate** (see page 79) down below facing onto the lake at the heart of the Barbican Centre. Take the stairs down to St Giles' – one of the few late medieval churches left in the City. Poet John Milton was buried in St Giles and Oliver Cromwell married here. The church also has strong links with William Shakespeare and his family.

When finished, retrace your steps back to Wood Street and stop to look at the Wren tower of **(9) St Alban Wood Street** (see page 170) that stands in the middle of the road. This is now perhaps the most extraordinary private residence in London! Continue past the tower along Wood Street (cross-ing over Gresham Street) until you reach

Cheapside. Turn left down Cheapside and you will see the familiar tower of **(10) St Mary le Bow** (see page 118) on the other side of the road. Any person claiming to be a Cockney must by tradition have been born within the sound of St Mary's famous bells. The church also houses an excellent vegetarian restau-rant in its crypt, reached through the main entrance. You can also visit a chapel in another part of the crypt reached via a well-hidden staircase on the south-east corner of the church. It faces onto a courtyard with a statue of the explorer Captain John Smith.

After visiting St Mary's head south down Bow Lane at the back of the church. At the very bottom of Bow Lane by the entrance to Mansion House tube station, you will see the unusual Gothic Wren tower of **(11) St Mary Aldermary** (see page 115). The tower has a unique fan-vaulted ceiling of a kind normally only found in cathedrals. When leaving St Mary Aldermary continue heading south down Bow Lane until you are on Queen Victoria Street/Cannon Street, then cross over and walk down Garlick Hill until you see Upper Thames Street ahead. Here you will find the church of **(12) St James Garlickhythe** (see page 87) with its distinctive statue of St James on the projecting church clock. This church is named after the imported garlic that was once loaded onto a harbour (or hythe) nearby. It is also known as 'Wren's lantern' because its typically large Wren windows result in the interior being superbly lit.

When leaving St James, turn east along Skinners Lane (parallel to Upper Thames Street) which soon becomes College Street. You will shortly find **(13) St Michael Paternoster Royal** (see page 133). This is home to the Mission to Seafarers and was once the local church of Sir Richard Whittington, the famous 'Dick Whittington' of the English pantomime.

After taking leave of St Michael's, turn left continuing down College Street. When you reach Dowgate Hill walk north up the hill away from Upper Thames Street until you again reach Cannon Street. Directly opposite you will see Walbrook. Cross over and walk up Walbrook until you reach the plain, ragstone exterior of **(14) St Stephen Walbrook** (see page 153) on the

right hand side. St Stephen's is regarded as perhaps Wren's finest City parish church, with a superb dome that served as a trial run for the dome of St Paul's. It also contains a controversial marble altar sculpted by Henry Moore and the original telephone that was used to start the Samaritans service.

Leave St Stephen's and turn north up Walbrook, bearing right again past Mansion House and onto Bank. Keep right and you will see King William Street and **(15) St Mary Woolnoth** (see page 127) situated prominently at the junction of King William Street and Lombard Street. St Mary's is an excellent example of the work of Wren's gifted assistant Nicholas Hawksmoor. The church's rector, John Newton, wrote *Amazing Grace*.

When leaving St Mary's continue down King William Street and very soon on the right hand side you come to Abchurch Lane. Walk down Abchurch Lane until you come out into the open space of Abchurch Yard. Here you will see **(16) St Mary Abchurch** (see page 111) where this walk ends. Wren's church is regarded by many as being the equal to St Stephen Walbrook, not least because of its beautifully painted dome and rich furnishings. Among the treasures is the only documented original Grinling Gibbons reredos.

Western Walk [Fleet Street to High Holborn]

This walk starts at St Dunstan in the West, nearest transport
Chancery Lane or Temple LU

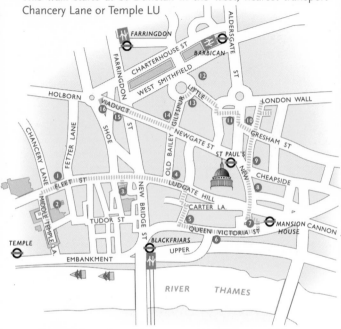

1. St Dunstan in the West
2. Temple Church
3. St Bride Fleet Street
4. St Martin within Ludgate
5. St Andrew by the Wardrobe
6. St Benet Paul's Wharf
7. St Nicholas Cole Abbey
8. St Augustine with St Faith
9. St Vedast alias Foster
10. St Anne and St Agnes
11. St Botolph without Aldersgate
12. St Bartholomew the Great
13. St Bartholomew the Less
14. St Sepulchre without Newgate
15. The City Temple
16. St Andrew Holborn

This walk starts at **(1) St Dunstan in the West** (see page 69), an excellent and rare example of early 19th-century City church architecture. Every 15 minutes the giants on its large clock strike one another. The statute of Elizabeth I on the right hand side was originally from the demolished city gate of Ludgate. Poet John Donne was once rector here and John Milton's *Paradise Lost* was published in the church grounds.

Standing under St Dunstan's looking onto Fleet Street, cross the road and walk west down Fleet Street. Again cross over and head down Middle Temple Lane (nearly opposite the entrance to Chancery Lane) and take the first main left following signs for Temple Church. **(2) Temple Church** (see page 160) is famous for being the spiritual home of the English Knights Templar. It is featured in the best-selling *The Da Vinci Code* and is now busier than ever. When leaving retrace your steps back onto Fleet Street and head east towards the City.

Before reaching the junction at Ludgate Circus, on the right hand side (near no.85 Fleet Street) is a small entrance. From here you can see **(3) St Bride's** (see page 59) just set back from Fleet Street. St Bride's has one of the oldest histories of any City church. Its Wren steeple famously inspired the design of the tiered wedding cake and it was also the family church of diarist Samuel Pepys. It is famous for being the 'journalists' church', continuing in this role even though the newspapers have largely abandoned Fleet Street.

When leaving St Bride's, turn back onto Fleet Street and head right over Ludgate Circus and up Ludgate Hill towards St Paul's. You will see about half way up Ludgate Hill the distinctive spire of **(4) St Martin within Ludgate** (see page 109). St Martin's was designed by Wren to be seen from an angle and to compliment the magnificent view of St Paul's. When finished at St Martin's you can either visit nearby St Paul's, or carry on further. To continue, cross over the road and walk about 50 metres along Ludgate Hill before heading south down the narrow Creed Lane. Take a left down Carter Lane, turning almost immediately right down St Andrew's Hill. Head down the hill until you meet Queen Victoria Street with Blackfriars Station to your right. Turn left (east) and on your left you will see **(5) St Andrew by the Wardrobe** (see page 33). The church gets its name from the King's wardrobe (or possessions) that were kept nearby. This was Wren's last, and cheapest, City parish church. Shakespeare lived nearby whilst working at his Blackfriars Theatre.

When finished, stay on this (northern) side of Queen Victoria Street and continue east. You will soon pass The College of Arms on your left, the centre for heraldry in the UK, and where Shakespeare applied with his father for a family coat of arms. Opposite on the southern side of Queen Victoria Street you will see the tower of **(6) St Benet Paul's Wharf** (see page 47). St Benet's is one of the least altered Wren churches in existence and is home to a Welsh congregation. When finished, continue east on the north side of Queen Victoria Street until on your left you find Wren's **(7) St Nicholas Cole Abbey** (see page 136), with St Paul's immediately behind. St Nicholas's is currently not open to the public. Walk past the church and take the steps immediately on your left up Old Fish Street Hill, which leads onto Distaff Lane. Continue straight on until

you reach a junction where you can see St Paul's on your left. Cross over the busy road onto New Change opposite. When walking up New Change, stop to look at the Wren tower of **(8) St Augustine with St Faith** (see page 170), now incorporated into the modern St Paul's Cathedral Choir School building.

Continue up New Change with St Paul's on your left until you reach Cheapside, with St Paul's tube station to your left. Cross over Cheapside, heading for the distinctive tower of Wren's **(9) St Vedast alias Foster** (see page 157) just down Foster Lane. If open, visit the pleasant courtyard inside the church grounds.

When finished, continue down Foster Lane until you reach Gresham Street. On the other side of this street you will see the redbrick exterior of Wren's **(10) St Anne and St Agnes** (see page 35), the only Lutheran church in the City, and noted for its excellent musical recitals. At this point you can take a detour down Noble Street that runs along the right hand side of St Anne and  St Agnes. On Noble Street take the first right onto Oat Lane. Here you will find a small garden and the foundations of St Mary Staining, a church first mentioned in the 12th century, but which was not rebuilt after the Great Fire of 1666. Continue on down Noble Street until you reach London Wall, and immediately on your right you will see the small garden and ruins of St Olave Silver Street, possibly the parish church William Shakespeare attended when he lived in Silver Street. St Olave's was also destroyed in the Great Fire and never rebuilt.

Back at St Anne and St Agnes, with your back to the entrance, turn right along Gresham Street until you meet St Martins Le Grand. Turn right and after about 100 metres along on the other side of the road you can see the olive green frontage of **(11) St Botolph without Aldersgate** (see page 49), just before the roundabout. Rarely open this small elegant church adjoins Postman's Park, a peaceful outdoor space that contains a wall of fascinating Victorian memorials to ordinary heroes.

Walk through Postman's Park to the exit on the far side, or alternatively, head in the same direction along narrow Little Britain which runs alongside St Botolph's. In either case you come out onto King Edward Street. You should then cross over and bear right until you see the entrance to Little Britain that continues on the other side of the road. Little Britain, described by Pip in Dickens' *Great Expectations* as a 'gloomy street', takes you up to the open space of West Smithfield (follow the signs for St Bartholomew's Hospital).

There are two churches to visit in this area – on the right under the Tudor timbered gatehouse **(12) St Bartholomew the Great** (see page 39), and on the left, just inside the entrance to St Bartholomew's Hospital, **(13) St Bartholomew the Less** (see page 43). St Bartholomew the Great is a magnificent building, famous for its Norman choir and the setting for many films, whilst St Bartholmew the  Less has served the patients and medical staff of London's oldest hospital for many centuries. Between the churches, look out on the walls of the hospital facing onto West Smithfield for memorials to Scotland's 'Braveheart' William Wallace and several Protestant martyrs, all of whom were publicly executed in this open space.

When finished, walk down Giltspur Street (reached by coming out of St Bartholomew's Hospital and turning left) until you see the distinctive scales of justice on top of Old Bailey. This is the former site of the infamous Newgate prison. On your right you can also see high up on an office block at the corner of Cock Lane a monument indicating where the Great Fire finally halted in 1666. The curious figure of the golden boy is explained because the Great Fire began in Pudding Lane and ended here at this corner which was then known as Pye (or Pie) Corner. This resulted in the belief that the fire was brought about because of divine retribution, the 'fat' boy signifying London's gluttony and sinfulness.

At the junction of Giltspur Street and Holborn Viaduct look right and immediately on your right the church of **(14) St Sepulchre without Newgate** (see page 150) can be seen. This was once the embarkation point for London's Crusaders in the Middle Ages, and was also at one time connected by an underground tunnel to Newgate Prison. When leaving St Sepulchre's turn right along Holborn Viaduct away from Old Bailey. Continue on for about 200 metres until you see the substantial, Italianate late Victorian frontage of the **(15) The City Temple (United Reformed Church)** on the left (see page 166). Just along from here on the same side you will find the Wren church of **(16) St Andrew Holborn** (see page 25). This was where Benjamin Disraeli was baptized and which also contains the tomb of Captain Thomas Coram, founder of London's famous Foundling Hospital. This is the last of the 16 City churches on the walk. Nearby Smithfields has numerous good eating places if you need a rest after your exertions.

Appendix

Wren Churches

Churches substantially unaltered:
St Benet Paul's Wharf, p.47
St Clement Eastcheap, p.65
St James Garlickhythe, p.87
St Margaret Lothbury, p.102
St Margaret Pattens, p.105
St Martin within Ludgate, p.109
St Mary Abchurch, p.111
Tower of St Mary Aldermary, p.115
St Michael Cornhill, p.129
St Peter upon Cornhill, p.147
St Stephen Walbrook, p.153

Renovated after Blitz to match original:
St Andrew by the Wardrobe, p.33
St Andrew Holborn, p.25
St Anne and St Agnes, p.35
St Bride's Fleet Street, p.59
St Edmund King and Martyr, p.75
St Lawrence Jewry, p.95
St Mary le Bow, p.118
St Mary at Hill, p.122
St Michael Paternoster Royal, p.133
St Nicholas Cole Abbey, p.136
St Vedast alias Foster, p.157
St Mary Aldermanbury (rebuilt in USA), p.168

Ruins or towers remaining:
St Magnus the Martyr – substantially altered, p.99
St Alban Wood St – tower, p.170
St Dunstan in the East – tower, p.170
St Mary Somerset – tower, p.171
St Olave Jewry – tower, p.171
Christ Church Newgate – tower & ruins, p.169
St Augustine with St Faith – tower, p.17

Demolished to make way for development:
All Hallows, Bread St, (dem. 1876-77)
All Hallows the Great, Lombard St, (dem. 1893-94)
All Hallows, Lombard St, (dem. 1939, tower now in Twickenham, UK)
St Antholin, Watling St (dem. 1875)
St Bartholomew, Exchange (dem. 1840-
St Benet Fink, Threadneedle St (dem. 1842-44)
St Benet, Gracechurch St (dem. 1867-6
St Christopher-le-Stocks, Threadneedle (dem. 1781)
St Dionis Backchurch, Fenchurch St (dem. 1878-79)
St George, Botolph Lane (dem. 1903-0
St Matthew, Friday St (dem. 1881)
St Michael, Bassishaw (dem. 1899)
St Michael, Crooked Lane (dem. 1831)
St Michael, Queenhithe (dem. 1876)
St Michael, Wood St (dem. 1894)
St Mildred, Poultry (dem. 1872)

Other:
St Mary Magdalene, Fish St (gutted by fire 1886, dem. 1887)

Useful Addresses

Friends of the City Churches
St Magnus the Martyr,
Lower Thames Street, London, EC3R 6DN;
Tel 020 7626 1555;
E-mail: friendsoflondoncitychurches@yahoo.co.uk;
Website: www.london-city-churches.org.uk
This voluntary organisation has done a great deal to conserve and promote the City Churches and provides staff to some of the churches to enable the churches to stay open to the public. The organisations website is a useful resource with events, maps, walks and contact details.

City Events
Website: www.cityevents.co.uk
A very useful website providing up-to-date information about the service times and concerts at the City churches. They also produce regular newsletters with news and views relating to the City Churches.

Corporation of London
www.cityoflondon.gov.uk/corporation
This website contains links to the Guildhall Library where many parish records are kept. You can also visit the Library at Aldermanbury EC2P 2EJ (020 7332 1868) which is next to St Lawrence Jewry.

City of London Churches
Website: www.cityoflondonchurches.com
The authors own website containing photographs and information on the city churches.

Steeljam
Website: www.steeljam.dircon.co.uk
Steeljam contains a great deal of useful genealogical information about the City churches on its website.

Glossary of Church Architecture

Apse - The domed or vaulted east end of a church.

Alter - The most sacred part of the church from where sermons and ceremonies conducted.

Baptistery - Area where fonts are stored and baptisms performed.

Bay - The divisions of a church marked by the interior supporting columns .

Bell Tower or Belfry - A tower where church bells were installed.

Boss - A rounded projection from the ceiling where the supporting arches of the roof meet.

Capital - The decorated top of a pillar.

Chancel - The Eastern part of a church including the Altar, the Choir, and the Sanctuary.

Chapel - A small place of worship set apart from the main church. The word chapel is also used to describe a Non-Conformist church and in some parts of the country a Roman Catholic church.

Choir - The area of a church dedicated to the choir. It is usually to the east of the Nave.

Clerestory - The highest level of windows above the aisle roof which allows extra light into the church.

Crossing - The central area where the choir, nave, and transepts meet.

Cruciform - A church designed in the shape of a cross.

Crypt - A vaulted chamber made to house graves and relics, generally located beneath the chancel.

Font - A basin on a pedestal that holds water for a baptism ceremony.

Gargoyle - A water-spout for draining a church roof carved into the shape of monsters or grotesque human faces.

Greek-cross Plan - Style of church with four equal arms.

Latin-cross Plan - Church plan with one arm longer than the other three.

Lectern - A reading desk designed to hold the Bible during services.

Misericord - A small shelf in the choir to enable the user to get some support while standing.

Nave - The main part of a church, where the congregation sits.

Orientation - The compass alignment of the church. The altar is usually oriented to the east.

Pew - Wooden seats or benches in the church.

Pulpit - A raised platform used for preaching and sometimes for leading prayers.

Reredos - A carved or painted wall behind an altar.

Rood - A carved cross erected at the entry to the chancel, often mounted on a 'rood-screen'.

Sanctuary - Where the high altar is placed.

Screen - A wall or fence that divides the church.

Spire - A tall conical structure on top of a church tower.

Stalls - A divisions within the choir, where clergy sat during the service.

Transepts - The wings that stick out at right angles to the main body of a church.

Triforium - The middle story of a church, above the Nave and below the Clerestory.

Vestry - A room set aside for putting on robes and where the vestments are kept.

Bibliography

The City of London Churches, *John Betjeman (1965)*
The City Churches, *Nikolaus Pevsner & Simon Bradley (1999)*
Survey of London, *John Stow (1598)*
The City Churches of Sir Christopher Wren, *Paul Jeffery (1996)*
England's Thousand Best Churches, *Simon Jenkins (2001)*
A Guide to the Architecture of London,
Edward Jones & Christopher Woodward (1983)
The London Encylopedia,
edited by Ben Weinreb and Christopher Hibbert (1983)

Index

A

Abbey of St Clare   p.4
All Hallows Barking   p.17
All Hallows Bread Street   p.158
All Hallows by the Tower   p.4-5, **17**, 77, 178
All Hallows on the Wall   p.**21**, 175
All Hallows Staining   p.22, **169**

B

Bach, Johann Sebastian   p.18, 36
Becket, Thomas á   p.99, 122, 179
Betjeman, John   p.54, 95, 115, 139
Blackfriars (religious order)   p.4
Blitz, The   p.10, 17, 54, 112, 170, 192
Brunel, Marc   p.26
Bulmer-Thomas, Ivor   p.34
Bunyan, John   p.36, 80
Butterfield, William   p.65, 75, 128, 133
Byfield, John   p.54, 58

C

Centre for Peace & Reconciliation p.176
Charles I   p.1, 30, 36, 91, 106, 136
Charles II   p.36, 47, 95, 143
Chippendale, Thomas   p.50
Christ Church Newgate   p.5, 10, **169**, 192
Churchill, Sir Winston   p.144, 167
City Events   p.11, 193
City of London Churches   p.193
City Temple, The (United Reformed Church)   p.**166,** 191
Condell, Henry   p.167, 182
Coram, Captain Thomas   p.26, 191
Corporation of London   p.95, 182, 193

Cromwell, Oliver   p.17, 79, 183
Crusades   p.72, 150, 160, 162, 191
Crutched Friars   p.4, 139, 177-178

D

Da Vinci Code   p.162, 187
George Dance the Elder   p.9, 21, 53, 57
George Dance the Younger   p.9, 21, 43, 49, 175
Defoe   p.1, 54, 80, 150
Dickens, Charles   p.6, 26, 69, 100, 124, 140, 148, 151, 178, 190
Disraeli, Benjamin   p.26, 165, 191
Dissolution of the Monasteries   p.5, 17, 40, 43, 53, 69, 109, 169, 176
Donne, John   p.70, 145, 187
Dutch Church, Austin Friars   p.4, 10, **72**, 175

E

Edward VI   p.72
Eliot, T S   p.179
Elizabeth I   p.44, 70, 84, 92, 96, 111, 169, 187
Evelyn, John   p.1, 6, 61

F

Foundling Hospital   p.26, 191
Franklin, Benjamin   p.40, 61
Friends of the City Churches   p.2, 11, 101, 193

G

Gibbons, Grinling   p.7, 18, 30, 50, 96, 102, 112, 116, 134, 137, 140, 145, 158, 185
Gold, James   p.9, 57, 175
Great Fire, The   p.6, 17-18, 25, 39, 49, 65, 69, 77, 99, 157, 179, 191

Greyfriars (religious order) p.4, 169
Guildhall Library p.95, 112, 167, 182, 193

H
Handel, George Frederick p.26, 162
Harris, Renatus p.18, 30, 54, 65, 79, 162
Hawksmoor, Nicholas p.7, 9, 75, 87, 127, 129, 133, 157, 170, 185
Hayward, John p.119, 134
Heminges, John p.167, 182
Henry I p.39, 91, 100
Henry VIII p.5, 20, 29, 33, 40, 43, 53-54, 77, 83, 88, 91, 169
Holborn Viaduct p.25, 27, 166, 191
Holman Hunt, William p.80, 145
Holy Trinity Minories p.10, 96
Hooke, Robert p.1, 7, 35, 47, 75, 102, 109, 147

J
James I p.30, 33, 161
James II p.106, 171
Jewin Welsh Presbyterian Church p.10, **166**
Jones, Inigo p.1, 6, 44, 48, 170
Journalists' Church p.61, 187
Judge Jeffreys p.1, 18, 162, 167

K
Keats, John p.58
Knighten Guild p.53
Knights Hospitaller p.160
Knights Templar p.4, 18, 160, 187

L
Laud, William (Bishop of London) p.6, 20, 91

M
Magna Carta p.70, 162
Marshall, Joshua p.150
Mendelssohn p.36, 102, 122, 148
Milton, John p.36, 61, 71, 80, 116, 183, 187
Monument p.179
Moore, Henry p.10, 145, 154, 185
More, Sir Thomas p.20, 29, 79, 96, 125
Musicians' Church p.151

N
Nelson, Lord p.144-145
Newgate prison p.21, 150, 191
Newton, John p.128, 185

P
Penn, William p.18, 150
Pepys, Samuel p.1, 6, 17, 61, 70, 139-141, 178, 187
Plague, The Great p.25, 54, 61, 80, 84, 141, 154
Postman's Park p.50, 190
Priory of St Bartholomew p.4
Priory of St Helen p.4, 83
Priory of the Holy Trinity p.4, 53, 91
Purcell, Henry p.66, 92, 129

Q
Queen Anne p.127, 144
Queen Elizabeth II p.144
Queen Mary I p.136
Queen Victoria p.48, 144

R
Rahere p.5, 39-40, 43-44
Reformation p.5-6, 8, 18, 72, 105, 111, 124-125
Richard II p.43, 100

Roman London p.1-4, 17, 21, 49, 59, 95, 118, 127, 147, 149, 182
Roman and Saxon Origins p.2
Roman Empire p.2-3, 83

S

Schmidt, Bernard p.92, 148, 162
Shakespeare, William p.1, 29, 33-34, 48, 57, 84, 167, 183
Sherrin, George p.9, 124
Shuttleworth, Henry p.136
Smith, Captain John p.110, 120, 151
Spanish and Portuguese Synagogue p.10, **165**, 177
St Alban Wood Street p.4, 10, **170**, 183, 192
St Andrea de Castello p.33
St Andrew Holborn p.**25**, 165, 191St Andrew Undershaft p.5-6, **29**, 176
St Andrew by the Wardrobe p.10, **33**, 188, 192
St Anne & St Agnes p.10, **35**, 158, 189, 192
St Augustine with St Faith p.10, **170**, 189, 192
St Bartholomew by the Exchange p.157
St Bartholomew the Great p.4-5, **39**, 151, 190
St Bartholomew the Less p.5, 9, **43**, 190
St Bartholomew's Hospital p.44, 116, 151, 190-191
St Benet Gracechurch Street p.140
St Benet Paul's Wharf p.**47**, 188, 192
St Botolph Aldgate p.9, p.**53**, 177
St Botolph Bishopsgate p.9, **57**, 175
St Botolph Aldersgate p.**49**, 190
St Bride's Fleet Street p.4, 10, 21, **59**, 119, 140, 187, 192

St Christopher le Stocks p.157
St Clement Eastcheap p.**65**, 171, 181, 192
St Dunstan in the East p.10, **170**, 178, 192
St Dunstan in the West p.9, **69**, 187
St Edmund King and Martyr p.4, **75**, 181, 192
St Ethelburga the Virgin p.5, 10, **77**, 176
St Giles Cripplegate p.5, **79**, 183
St Helen Bishopsgate p.4-5, **83**, 176, 182
St James Garlickhythe p.**87**, 184, 192
St Katherine Cree p.5-6, 29, **91**, 177
St Lawrence Jewry p.**95**, 182, 192
St Magnus the Martyr p.**99**, 128, 179, 192
St Margaret Lothbury p.**102**, 182, 192
St Margaret Pattens p.**105**, 179, 192
St Martin Orgar p.**171**
St Martin Ludgate p.8, **109**, 188, 192
St Mary Abchurch p.7-8, **111**, 153, 185, 192
St Mary Aldermanbury p.10, **167**, 182, 192
St Mary Aldermary p.8, **115**, 184, 192
St Mary le Bow p.4, 10, 48, **118**, 120, 157, 183, 192
St Mary at Hill p.10, **122**, 179, 192
St Mary le Grand p.4
St Mary Magdalene Fish St p.22, 192
St Mary Moorfields p.9, **124**
St Mary Somerset p.**171**, 192
St Mary Staining p.189
St Mary Woolnoth p.9, **127**, 185
St Matthew Friday Street p.34, 157
St Michael Cornhill p.9, **129**, 181, 192
St Michael Paternoster Royal p.**133**, 184, 192

St Michael Wood Street   p.36
St Mildred Bread Street   p.10
St Nicholas Cole Abbey   p.**136**, 147, 188, 192
St Olave Hart Street   p.6, **139**, 178
St Olave Jewry   p.102, **171**, 192
St Olave Silver Street   p.189
St Paul's Cathedral   p.3, 7, 106, **143**, 153, 170, 189
St Peter upon Cornhill   p.2, 102, **147**, 181, 192
St Sepulchre Newgate   p.8, **150**, 191
St Stephen Coleman   p.10
St Stephen Walbrook   p.8, 10, **153**, 184, 192
St Swithin Cannon Street   p.10
St Vedast alias Foster   p.**157**, 189, 192
Steeljam   p.193
Stone, Nicholas   p.6, 30
Stow, John   p.30, 99, 122, 147, 176

T
Templar knights   p.17, 58, 160, 187
Temple Church   p.4, **160**, 187
Throckmorton, Sir Nicholas   p.92, 177
Tyburn   p.77, 151

U
Union of Benefices Act   p.9, 147, 171

V
Van Gogh   p.72, 175
Vanbrugh, Sir John   p.7, 154

W
Wallace, William   p.40, 190
Watts' Cloister   p.50
Wellington, Duke of   p.144-145
Wesley, John   p.36, 84

Whittington, Dick   p.119, 133, 184
William the Conqueror   p.33, 65, 153
Wood, Sir Henry   p.151
Wren, Sir Christopher   p.1, 6-7, 9, 33, 59, 106, 111, 136, 143, 145, 148, 157, 170, 181-182, 184-185, 187-188

Order our other Metro Titles

The following titles are also available from Metro Publications. Please send your order along with a cheque made payable to Metro Publications to the address below. **Postage and packaging free.**

Alternatively call our customer order line on **020 8533 7777** (Visa/Mastercard/Switch), Open Mon-Fri 9am-6pm

Metro Publications
PO Box 6336, London N1 6PY
info@metropublications.com
www.metropublications.com

London Market Guide
Andrew Kershman
£6.99 ISBN 1-902910-14-1

Bargain Hunters' London
Andrew Kershman
£6.99 ISBN 1-902910-15-X

Food Lovers' London
Jenny Linford
£8.99 ISBN 1-902910-22-2

London Theatre Guide
Richard Andrews
£7.99 ISBN 1-902910-08-7

Veggie & Organic London
Russell Rose
£6.99 ISBN 1-902910-21-4

Book Lovers' London
Lesley Reader
£8.99 ISBN 1-902910-26-5

**Museums & Galleries
of London**
Abigail Willis
£8.99 ISBN 1-902910-20-6

London Architecture
Marianne Butler
£8.99 ISBN1-902910-18-4

London's Cemeteries
Darren Beach
£6.99 ISBN 1-902910-23-0

London's Parks and Gardens
Nana Ocran
£6.99 ISBN 1-902910-19-2

London's City Churches
Stephen Millar
£6.99 ISBN 1-902910-24-9